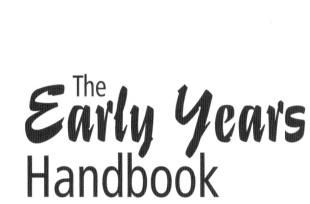

The Early Years Handbook

**support for practitioners in
the foundation stage**

Editor: **Max de Bóo**

The Early Years Handbook

support for practitioners in the foundation stage

Editor: **Max de Bóo**

the curriculum partnership

the curriculum partnership

The Curriculum Partnership is an informal grouping of the larger subject teaching associations. We are working together in areas where collaboration serves the profession better than our individual efforts, and one of the first fruits of our collaboration is this handbook. Written by early years subject experts (from the GA, MA, ASE, NATE and DATA), the treatment is entirely holistic in nature and has been skilfully blended into an easily accessible guide for foundation stage practitioners. Underpinning it is the belief of all the contributors in a play-based approach to early learning.

The book consists of an introduction and twelve themes; the introduction explains the pedagogy underpinning the project, and the themes are play-based approaches. They cover all the early learning goals, in an imaginative and enjoyable way, and prepare children for the more subject-oriented work they will encounter in key stage 1.

The Association for Science Education (ASE - www.ase.org.uk)

The Design and Technology Association (DATA - www.data.org.uk)

The Geographical Association (GA - www.geography.org.uk)

The Mathematics Association (MA - www. ma.org.uk)

The National Association of Teachers of English (NATE - www.nate.org.uk)

Design: Bryan Ledgard Publishing Design & Photography, Sheffield, UK
Editing: Philip Gardner, Asgard Publishing, Leeds, UK
Printed in China through Colorcraft Ltd.,Hong Kong

ISBN 1 84377 115 2
First published 2004
Impression number 10 9 8 7 6 5 4 3 2 1
Year   2007   2006   2005

Published by the Geographical Association, 160 Solly Street, Sheffield S1 4BF.
(Website: www.geography.org.uk; E-mail: ga@geography.org.uk)
The Geographical Association is a registered charity: no 313129

contributors

Clare Benson is Professor of Education (design and technology) and director of CRIPT at the University of Central England, and Chair of the Primary Advisory Group for the Design and Technology Association.

Varsha Chudasama was a nursery teacher at Pinner Park First School, Harrow, and is now Foundation Stage Curriculum Leader at the Hillview Centre in Harrow.

Barbara Conridge is Education for English in Bedfordshire and Chair of the Primary Committees at the National Association for the Teaching of English.

Max de Bóo is a Consultant in Primary Science and Early Years Education and a member of the Publications Committee at the Association for Science Education.

Rosemary Feasey is a Consultant in Primary Science and a former Chair of the Association for Science Education.

Jane Johnston is a Senior Lecturer in Education at Bishop Grosseteste College, Lincoln, and a long-standing member of the Association for Science Education.

Lynne McClure works with teachers and trainee teachers in primary and secondary schools. She is an active member of both ATM and MA, which includes editing the Mathematical Associations Primary Mathematics journal.

Paula Owens is Deputy Head at Eastchurch Primary School and a PhD research student at Canterbury Christ Church College. She is a member of the Primary and Middle School Section Committee of the GA and was a member of the Early Years Working Party that produced the recent GA Early Years Strategy.

Margaret Perkins is Lecturer in Literacy Education in the Institute of Education, University of Reading, and member of the Primary Committee of the National Association for the Teaching of English.

Maggie Rogers is Co-ordinator of Primary Design and Technology Education in the Department of Educational Studies at Goldsmiths' College, University of London, and a member of the Primary Advisory Group at the Design and Technology Association.

acknowledgements

We are deeply indebted to all the staff in the early years settings who collaborated with us: our thanks for their ideas, support, and permission to photograph and record the children's voices.

The following nursery schools and individuals deserve a special mention for their general support of activities featured in this handbook and/or specifically for the supply of images:

- the staff and pupils of Eastchurch Church of England Primary School, Isle of Sheppey, Kent (www.eastchurch.kent.sch.uk), especially Mel Ryan, Chris Ford, Anne Dawson and Sarah James
- Karen Disspain (Headteacher) and Nina Mistry, and all the 'child care' students on placement at Pinner First School Nursery, Harrow during 2002-03
- Hazel Yeomans (Headteacher) and Hilary O'Byrne (Education Excellence Co-ordinator) at Hillview Centre, South Harrow
- Denby Street Nursery and Family Centre, Sheffield
- Diane Swift, GA Valuing Places Project Manager
- Barbara Reilly-O'Donnell at St Thomas More RC Primary School, Belmont, Durham
- Suzanne Prudhoe, Westgate Hill Primary School, Newcastle-upon-Tyne
- Melanie Mercer and children at Husbourne Crawley Primary School, Bedfordshire
- Tricia Kraftl and children at Wootton St Peters Primary School, Abingdon
- The Nursery, Grimes Dyke Primary School, Leeds for the spider painting on page 20
- Josie and Theo for the work that appears on pages 48, 64 and 82
- Peter for the work that appears on pages 48 and 75
- Elaine Wilford for helpful suggestions on drafts of each theme
- Margaret MacCormack and the children of Potton Lower School, Bedfordshire
- Janet Hill from World Education Development Group (WEDG) and UNICEF
- Alumwell Nursery School, Walsall
- Gill Wilkes, Sue Shaw and all at South Ascot Pre-School

The Geographical Association also wishes to thank Kathy Alcock, Kate Dean, Elaine Jackson, Liz Lewis, Margaret Mackintosh, Fran Martin, Paula Richardson, for their contributions to the development of the GA's Early Years Strategy in general and Handbook in particular.

contents

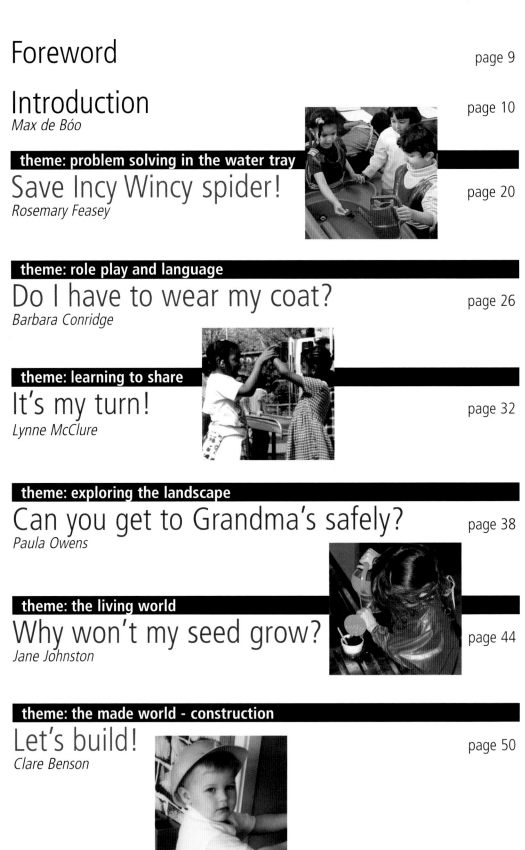

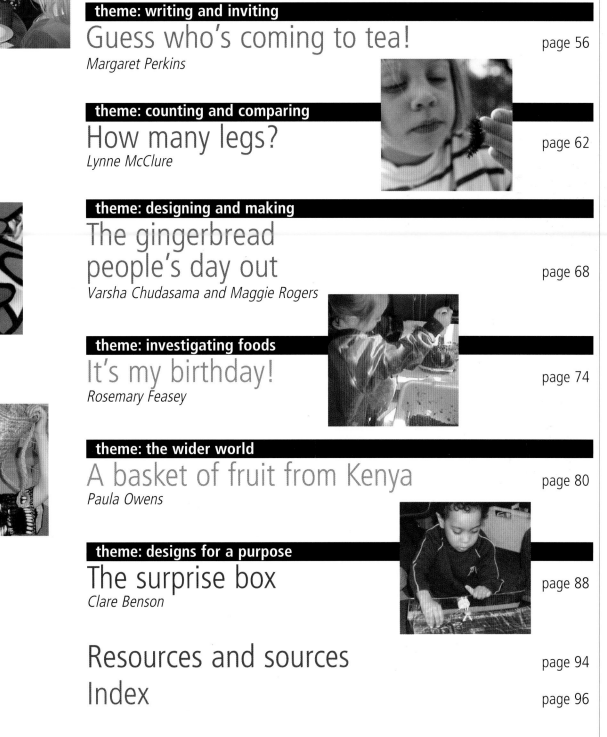

foreword

Rt Hon Margaret Hodge MBE MP

Minister for Children, Young People and Families

Children's early learning experiences are key to their attainment in later life. During this time, children develop rapidly - physically, intellectually, emotionally and socially. Good quality early education offers children the opportunity to reach their full potential and provides a solid framework for later learning.

Children learn best in safe and secure environments; and through enjoyment, challenge and play. These are amongst the principles of the Foundation Stage curriculum for three to five year olds. The Foundation Stage has been part of the national curriculum since 2002 and has been warmly welcomed across a diverse sector. With free, universal early education now available for all three and four year olds, children can access the Foundation Stage in a wide range of settings, including playgroups, childminder networks, daycare nurseries, nursery schools, nursery classes and reception classes in primary schools.

The government is also working to support the integration of high quality early education and childcare with health and family services. By 2008, we aim to have designated 1700 children's centres in England, providing a high quality integrated service to children aged from birth to 5 and their families in the 20% most disadvantaged wards.

The Foundation Stage has an important role to play in these plans, setting out the guiding principles for children's early learning experiences and creating a framework within which children are offered the opportunity to reach their full potential. It is vital that we all continue to raise the quality of Foundation Stage delivery, across all settings and for every child. I therefore welcome this *Early Years Handbook* which aims to do just that and which links closely to the Foundation Stage curriculum.

I am delighted that a group of Subject Associations have worked together to produce this holistic perspective on Foundation Stage learning. Subject Associations provide a great deal of support for practitioners right across the curriculum and for all age groups. Bringing that support for different subjects together is an important step forward. I am very pleased to see this handbook and I am sure it will prove useful.

Editor: Max de Bóo

introduction

I collected my tray, joined the queue at the conference cafeteria and found myself eavesdropping on a junior teacher speaking to a reception teacher.

Junior teacher: *Oh, come on! Holistic education is like old-fashioned topic work – nobody really knows what the children are learning. We need to teach separate subjects in separate slots.*

Reception teacher: *Not necessarily. Children learn what is right for them at the time in a particular context – like us picking and choosing at this buffet dinner. We still get the nourishment we need and we enjoy eating. If we were always forced to eat meat and two veg. when we just fancied salad, we wouldn't enjoy it, or we would leave it on our plate, or even sick it up later!*

Junior teacher: *No, no. We just have to make the meat and two veg. really tasty.*

Reception teacher: *But the fact remains – I don't always want meat and two veg. Sometimes I just want a salad ... or a bowl of soup with a roll.*

Junior teacher: *But meat and two veg. is good for you!*

The teachers departed with a variety of food on their trays and I took my chicken salad and joined my own colleagues.

Holistic education or separate subjects?

In truth, there is some value in both the points of view expressed here. There are times when we need to focus our teaching on specific areas to develop children's skills. Specifying learning objectives helps our planning and ensures that we offer children a broad, balanced curriculum. This is one of the purposes underpinning the *Curriculum Guidance for the Foundation Stage* (hereafter referred to as *Curriculum Guidance*): dividing the early years curriculum into six areas enables us to use it as 'a framework to plan the learning environment, activities and experiences' (QCA, 2000, p. 5).

Nevertheless, young children learn in a much more eclectic, holistic way. They do not see the distinction between 'work' and 'play', between language development and scientific exploration. Their cognitive learning is bound up with their emotional learning (Beetlestone, 1998). Their learning does not occur in

a structured, linear way. We can stimulate and guide children's learning, but in the event they will focus on what is important, interesting or significant to them at that time (de Bóo, 1999).

This alternative view of how young children learn is endorsed by *Curriculum Guidance* itself in its statement that '*all* of young children's learning [cannot] be divided into areas.' (QCA, 2000, p. 25). Language and mathematical skills and knowledge are integral to most of the work we do with young children; motor skills and scientific knowledge are learned while designing and making; personal and social skills while choosing seats in the role-play 'bus'. In short, we may think of the curriculum as 'everything children do, see, hear or feel in their setting, both planned and unplanned' (QCA, 2000, p. 5).

Nevertheless, statutory national criteria have forced us to 'adjust to a [more sharply-focused curriculum] than has occurred in the past. We now have to define more precisely what we do' (Moyles, 1996, p. 90). The six key areas of experience defined by *Curriculum Guidance* (QCA, 2000) that are considered essential to the education of young children are:

- Personal, social and emotional development (PSE)
- Communication, language and literacy
- Mathematical development
- Knowledge and understanding of the world
- Physical development
- Creative development

Within these areas are recognisable subdivisions to ensure that children are taught a range of skills and ideas – for example, 'design and technology' is included in 'Knowledge and understanding of the world', and 'music' within 'Creative development'.

The daily experiences which provide the context for the learning include:

- Sand
- Water
- Outdoor play
- Role play
- Construction
- Art materials
- Exploration areas
- Writing provision
- Spatial awareness
- Table-top play
- Small world play
- Print environment

It is perfectly possible to provide young children with access to the whole curriculum by using a themed or topic approach, as long as we evaluate the learning opportunities within the framework of each theme, and, where one element receives less emphasis, we compensate for it in the next theme (Moyles, 1996). Reflection and evaluation help us to maintain a balance. Fortunately, throughout the varied experiences in each theme, there are many 'transferable skills (observing, problem-solving, communicating, social and motor skills) and thinking processes (predicting, speculating, evaluating)' (Boorman and Rogers, 2000, p. 40).

For example, the children designing vehicles for the gingerbread people (pages 68-73) were using critical evaluation and problem-solving skills: 'This is not good glue! I'll use sticky tape'.

Children's prior experiences

Adopting a themed approach values the range of prior experiences and skills, cultural expectations and belief systems that children bring to the learning environment. For example, children have intuitive ideas about shape and symmetry, reflected in their early pictorial drawings. In the vignette below, Tom lacked words but not understanding, and Theo was horrified at the idea that 'men' might have babies. The children variously showed knowledge of size and capacity (filling up), plant cycles and seasonal change, and human reproduction. Their discussion showed good use of spoken and body language/communication, reasoning and explaining, and the need for a key word – 'bigger'.

I was exploring and discussing foods with young reception children. I asked:

Teacher: *What happens to the food inside?*

[Tom points to his feet.]

Alex: *Yes, and then the more you eat it gets up and up to there* [points to his neck].

Theo: *The more you eat, it goes down to there* [feet] *and you get big and big* [demonstrates getting bigger and bigger].

Teacher: *You get bigger?* [Nods from the children.] *So you grow and grow and grow?*

Theo: *Until the winter stops you.*

Bansi: *If you eat a lot, you get a baby out of your stomach.*

Theo: *Only ladies!*

Teacher: *What makes you think that?*

Bansi: *Well my Mummy eats a lot and she's growing a baby in her stomach.*

When we present children with new tasks they use their prior experiences to interpret and complete these tasks. For example, geographical knowledge has a personal, unique relevance to each child. In Selley (1999), young children were asked to draw a 'map' of their journey to school. One child drew the interior of her parent's car; another child drew just the bridge she crossed with boats below, and a third child noted the noises and smells of the journey.

It is not always easy to appreciate the breadth of perspectives that young children have from their existing experiences – this is one of the aspects that makes teaching young children both daunting and delightful. We are always trying to find the balance between not underestimating a child's early capabilities and not overestimating the child's transferable skills and knowledge.

For example, a colleague and I had just finished working with 3–4-year-old children on the theme of 'Humpty Dumpty'. We now had a papier maché'd Humpty sitting on a wall made of cereal packets stuck together. We stood admiring the result. The nursery teacher said, 'It's just a pity the wall's not level.' Stavros paused as he hurtled past. 'No,' he said, 'castle wall.' The children, unknown to us, had been building a *crenellated* castle wall!

Valuing children's existing experiences as the starting-point for learning is described as the constructivist approach – that is, constructing or developing new ideas from the children's existing experiences, rather than assuming an absence of skills or knowledge. Then children have a 'preparedness' for learning that we call the 'zone of proximal development'. This is the notion put forward by Vygotsky, that the children's learning zone 'defines those functions that have not yet matured but are in the process of maturation,

functions that will mature tomorrow but are currently in an embryonic state. These functions should be termed the "buds" or "flowers" of development rather than the "fruits" of development' (1978, p. 86).

This zone may not be the same for every child, but there is a potential within each child that with appropriate stimuli and support, or 'scaffolding' (Bruner and Haste, 1993), they can develop their current capabilities to the full. But what constitutes 'appropriate stimuli and support'?

The importance of child-initiated play

We can argue that, first and foremost, the stimulus for learning in the early years setting is one where children have opportunities to learn through play or playful exploration. Such an environment values child-initiated activities as well as those planned and provided by the adult practitioners. It can require courage to allow children to play. Student teachers surveyed by Moyles thought that 'children are only learning when [we] are teaching ... concepts that the lesson [has] been designed to "cover".' (1996, p. 41).

However, we know from substantial research that 'children are much more involved in the task, and more competent in devising and using strategies, when they work on problems that they themselves have set. Young children can be ingenious and inventive in defining a variety of tasks, in directing their own activities with a high degree of motivation and in correcting their errors' (Bruner and Haste, 1993, p. 13). Children at play can encourage other children to become involved in that play (e.g. page 58). Furthermore, child-initiated play

encourages positive attitudes and self-esteem as well as teaching and testing 'higher-order thinking skills ... decision-making and individualised learning, and is self-motivating' (de Bóo, 1999, p. 134). For example, the children setting off on their travels (page 27) set up a row of chairs to simulate a bus, swayed together as they went round the bends in the road, with the 'driver' calling 'Watch out!'

Adult support

Adult support is essential for children to feel confident in 'playing'. First and foremost adults provide an environment that is safe. Then children come from a variety of backgrounds ... with no or many siblings, an absent parent or a live-in extended family. Practitioners teach the children that they are valued as individuals and that sharing and co-operating lead to feeling good and having fun. Children learn how to develop positive relationships with adults beyond their own family circle. We know that 'more affectionate, communicative and responsive adult–child interactions are related to better language development' (Melhuish and Moss, 1990, p. 12).

Furthermore, play does not exist in the absence of familiar and new materials and phenomena, indoors and outdoors. This has implications for imaginative resourcing by the practitioners. Support for children's play could mean changing the sand in the tray from dry to wet to spark new interest, adding new clothes to the role-play area, or freezing ice balloons for exploration, prompting curiosity, enthusiasm and fresh ideas for play. Establishing an interesting outdoor environment can 'provide a sensory environment where children are exposed to

changes in light, temperature and elements of the weather, and to a range of auditory and visual images. The visual perspective is wider ... and ... creative thought flourishes' (Beetlestone, 1998, p. 124). Well-organised resources that are easily accessible support the development of decision-making, exploration and responsibility. 'This allows practitioners to work alongside children, to value what they are doing and to interact appropriately to support development and learning, rather than simply managing resources' (QCA, 2000, p. 20).

Support for, or 'scaffolding', children's self-initiated play requires an environment of good communication and productive questions (see below).

Directed activities

Child-initiated play is invaluable, but children will always need activities planned and directed by adults if they are to develop their knowledge and skills across the curriculum. *Curriculum Guidance* recognises that 'children need activities planned by adults as well as those that children plan or initiate themselves' (QCA, 2000, p. 11). Directed activities allow practitioners to help children to 'make connections in their learning ... and to reflect on what they have ... learnt' (QCA, 2000, p. 22). Directed activities ensure that children have learning opportunities that might not arise in spontaneous play. Directed activities will provide for indoor and outdoor play, make provision for individual needs, and encourage progress in learning.

There are certain skills and aspects of knowledge that need to be taught specifically such as new and relevant vocabulary, (the) spatial concepts of squares and triangles, time concepts of last week and next year, (and) or

scientific skills of predicting and explaining why 'solid' birthday candles go 'runny' when they melt. 'Directed activities [can] focus the children's attitudes on the learning of different techniques [and strategies], which, in turn, frees them to play and recreate with increased knowledge, skills and understanding' (Moyles, 1996, p. 79). For example, the introduction of the drainpipe into the water tray (page 22) transformed the children's play and challenged their thinking and problem-solving skills.

Adult direction is also vital in providing children with challenges, whether in planned activities or child-initiated play. Challenges can occur in two ways – productive questioning during play, and providing set challenges.

Productive questions

Good questions will not diminish the children's play but can encourage thinking skills, language, problem-solving and co-operation. Certain types of question are essential in extending and enriching the nature of children's play. Productive questions are usually open-ended or person-centred rather than object-centred or closed questions. For example, in 'Do I have to wear my coat?' (pages 26-31), the question 'What will you need to take with you?' (open, person-centred] has several satisfactory, optional answers), and several children can respond with confidence (e.g. jacket, suitcase, sandwiches, toy, sunglasses). The question 'Is it hot or cold in Switzerland?' (object-centred, closed) requires a one-word reply and prior knowledge. Only children who have actually visited Switzerland or have family there would feel confident in replying.

Additionally, the open-ended questions 'Or ... ?' and 'Anything else?' imply that other responses would be welcome too, so that children can respond by adding information or ideas, or by elaborating on their previous responses (de Bóo, 1999).

Productive questions can also provide a challenge to children's thinking (see below).

Note: A selection of these questions could be used as the basis for a discussion between all the practitioners involved in working with the children, considering the thought-processes being encouraged, the possible responses of the children, and possible next steps.

Set challenges

These are the kind of challenges which pose a problem to solve, such as on page 83: 'Can you make a basket like Handa's?', or 'Can you make some fruits for Handa's basket?'. As Fisher stated: 'Problem-solving activities will stimulate and develop skills of thinking and reasoning. They utilise and make relevant the child's knowledge of facts and relationships. Getting results helps develop confidence and capability, the "I-can-think-this-out-for-myself" attitude. It can also provide opportunities for children to share ideas and to learn to work effectively with others, the "Let's-work-this-out-together" approach. There is no better way to check if a child understands a process or a body of knowledge than to see if he [sic] can use that understanding in the solving of a problem' (1994, p. 98).

Responding to challenges involves creative imagination, personal expression, application of prior knowledge and experience, and, very often, the need for co-operation with others.

Adult direction is not only important in providing set challenges but also in devising the extent of the challenge. Challenges need to be set in a context that is familiar. Children are better able to design and make a 'spider's web' in the classroom when they have actually seen a real one, explored string and wool, and used card and gluesticks confidently. Children can draw a spider on screen more confidently when they have observed spiders closely (pages 21 and 24), discussed the shape of their bodies and the number of legs and used a suitable software package before. All of these skills need to be taught directly.

Moreover, set challenges need to be 'on such a scale that they provide cognitive dissonance and encourage thinking skills, without being so challenging that they cause a lack of confidence and a loss of self-esteem' (Siraj-Blatchford and MacLeod-Brudenell, 1999, p. 29). Children who are left to themselves 'are not very good at bringing their previous experience to bear on solving related problems' (Fisher, 1994, p. 29). Adults need to be ready to listen, praise and advise. In such a supportive environment, children who are successful in meeting challenges become confident learners, willing to take further risks in problem-solving, and 'view practitioners as helpful teachers' (QCA, 2000, p. 21).

Encouraging positive attitudes

Over the last two decades, government documentation has alternated between emphasising and ignoring the importance of children's attitudes. Perhaps this area of teaching is perceived to be difficult, as attitudes can be 'complex and ... overlap ... with all aspects of life' (Johnston, 1996, p. 103). Attitudes are difficult to assess in a formal way, especially by external assessment techniques. Nevertheless, *Curriculum Guidance* recommends that children should acquire 'positive attitudes and dispositions towards their learning' (QCA, 2000, p. 8) and other government documents now emphasise the role of positive attitudes in educating young people for citizenship. Those of us working with young children have never stopped valuing this aspect of learning. We have always known that the development of positive attitudes is as essential to learning as skills and knowledge. Such attitudes include:

- Co-operation with others
- Creativity and inventiveness
- Critical reflection
- Curiosity
- Enthusiasm
- Independence
- Open-mindedness
- Leadership
- Perseverance

Positive attitudes to particular subject areas:

- Problem solving
- Respect for evidence
- Responsibility
- Self-confidence/self-esteem
- Sensitivity to living things
- Volunteering information and ideas
- Willingness to tolerate uncertainty

Most of these attitudes are reflected in the six areas of learning as defined by the QCA's *Curriculum Guidance* (2000), for example, co-operation with others and independence (Personal, social and emotional), volunteering information and ideas (Communication, language and literacy) and respect for evidence (Knowledge and understanding of the world).

There is only one real way in which we can encourage children's positive attitudes, and that is by modelling those attitudes ourselves. Young children will learn to show curiosity and enthusiasm themselves when they see *us* excited about a woodlouse crawling across a leaf; they will learn that uncertainty is acceptable when they discover that *we* are afraid of the dark; they will learn that working together is best when they see teacher and classroom assistant co-operating to solve a problem.

And there is only one way in which attitudes can be assessed – by practitioners observing the children's behaviour. This underlines the importance of regular and individual comments in children's profiles (see below). Parents and children can feel proud when they are told of 'Sarah's perseverance' and 'Sanjeev's responsible behaviour'.

For example, in 'Why won't my seed grow?' (pages 44-49), Suzanne remembered to check the seeds each day to see if they had enough water (responsible behaviour: caring for living things).

Communication in the early years

'Three-year-old Minnie rushed into the nursery and clung to my leg. She was not able to tell me in words what was going on but I knew what she was feeling. She remained clinging to my leg all day.'

Practitioners working with young children become adept at interpreting what is happening to their charges: a flushed face, a silent withdrawal, an overheard 'You be the driver, then' or 'Look what I've done!'

An early years setting is rich in communication – between child and child, and between children and adults. Young children are just beginning to make sense of what people mean by using 'a range of cues ... such as the context of the discussion, gestures and movements, and the use of vocabulary within the sentence construction' (Donaldson, 1987, p. 38).

Children develop most effectively in an environment where *their* communication is valued and where we make our intentions and ideas very clear. As Moyles states, we 'must value children's communication in the classroom context, not just those occasions when children are responding to the teacher but when children are exploring ideas and mental images of their own through personal and individual dialogue with the teacher or with other children' (1996, p. 43). Once again, this is endorsed by *Curriculum Guidance*: 'Conversation, open-ended questions and thinking out loud are important tools in developing vocabulary and challenging thinking' (QCA, 2000, p. 23).

However good we are at intuiting children's non-verbal communication, we do want to develop their spoken language. We can model the exploration of ideas in our speech by using phrases such as 'I wonder if ...' and 'I wonder what would happen if ...'. We can support or scaffold children's use of new vocabulary by modelling the use of key words in our own speech – for example, by using everyday words and scientific terms in tandem (e.g. see-through and transparent), until children are confident in their use of the scientific term (Feasey, 1999, 2000).

New vocabulary can only be acquired in a meaningful way if presented in a relevant context. Donaldson (1987) describes this as language being 'embedded' – in other words, language out of context is difficult to understand or meaningless. The truth of this has been brought home to me on several occasions!

By going into didactic mode (that is, '*I*

This conversation occurred after we had just returned from a trip to the local park with the 5–6-year-olds, having explored trees and plants, the little stream and other features:

Jennifer: *We tried to cross the river.*

Teacher: *Did you?*

Jennifer: *But we couldn't get over.*

Teacher: *So how do you think we could cross the river?*

Jennifer: *Bridge.*

Chris: *Or cut the tree down and walk across.*

Teacher: *Or?*

Lisa: *Put welly boots on.*

George: *If it was a thin part you could jump it but if it's a wide part you'd fall in.*

Teacher: *Does anybody know the name of a place where it is shallow enough to walk across?*

[Silence from all the children. Finally a few murmur 'No'.]

Teacher: *The word is 'ford'. A ford ... is where it's so shallow that ...*

Alan: *Ford Fiesta.*

Teacher: *Pardon?*

Alan: *Ford Fiesta.*

Teacher: *Yes, well the name 'ford' ...*

I bumbled on for a few more seconds before bringing the discussion back to the children's own personal and more relevant experiences!

know a word I am going to tell you even if it is completely irrelevant!') I shut down the conversation, and Alan quickly put me right!

In real life we don't actually need a sledge-hammer to crack a nut. 'Children are quick to infer meaning from contexts. [In normal life] ... we do not attempt to make sense of words in isolation' (Donaldson, 1987, p. 104). We can help children to acquire new vocabulary by modelling it in context and by 'reassuring children when they explore the meanings of new words themselves ... praising their use of "have-a-go" words and speech patterns rather than telling children they are "wrong"' (QCA, 2000, p. 23). Children will often 'think out loud', exploring speech and vocabulary. All they need from us is a little patience, and, where necessary, for us to supply the word that they are seeking (e.g. the word 'bigger' in the dialogue on page 11).

On other occasions, we can elaborate on the children's meaning: 'I see you've joined them together. You fixed that brick onto that one really well'. Giving children key words in meaningful contexts expands their repertoire of useful vocabulary.

In adult discussions, we take it for granted that we clarify or negotiate meanings. It is the same with children. Meanings are negotiated between adult and child and the very negotiation sends a message to the child that communication is a shared experience in which [the child] plays an important role (Bruner and Haste, 1993).

Most of all, we need to present children with further opportunities to practise this new vocabulary or hear it again. Key words heard at the time, even in a meaningful activity, constitute 'present-moment embedding'. 'The next step comes with extension into the past and into the future, but still the focus is on the personal life-plans, memories, hopes and fears' (Donaldson, 1987, p. 126).

Recognising children's achievements

In an early years setting, practitioners are giving positive approval most of the time by look, smile, nod and word. Recognition of achievement is easier and more purposeful when we:

(a) know the child (an ongoing process), and
(b) know what we are looking for (child development as defined in national documents).

'Significant achievement' can be recognised when children's 'responses reveal [their] skills, knowledge or attitudes, or when they respond in a way that is new for them – volunteering information, asking a question, offering support to another child' (Hutchin, 1999, p. 18).

Curriculum Guidance suggests that 'Information about children's learning [can be] gathered in a variety of ways, including recordings (models, paintings, designs, drawings, "writings", photographs and videos)' (QCA, 2000, p. 24). However, the most important method of recognising children's significant achievements is by *observation*. 'Observation of children when they are absorbed in a task is most revealing – their skills, ideas and attitudes, and capacity for learning. [This] can produce the most useful information, especially as to concepts, knowledge and ... gives an over-all profile of the child' (Moyles, 1996, p. 125).

Observation encompasses not only what children do but also what they say. Children's verbal responses are immensely important in revealing their prior experiences, knowledge and understanding, feelings, attitudes and skills.

Recording

What children say is so important that we need to devise strategies to record this on a regular basis. The advantages and disadvantages of four strategies are shown in Figure 1 below.

The reality of an early years setting probably means we have to use a range of the above strategies, but the dividends are enormous – we learn so much about individuals and groups of children.

Generally, information gathered about children's achievements is written into individual profiles. The task of structured recording can be streamlined by:

• designating who will observe, the length of time for observing and the observations will be recorded
• choosing specific (limited) achievements to look for, such as:
   • attitudes of co-operation and independence, *or*
   • skills of predicting and explaining, *or*
   • knowledge of place or number.

Inevitably, other curricular learning will occur, but specifying which achievements to watch out for concentrates our attention on specific aspects – just as in a busy urban environment it is easier to watch out for a no. 17 bus than to notice and recall *all* the buses, taxis and other vehicles passing by. This won't stop us noticing something special happening for an individual child, however. For example, while recording that most children are observing the flowers closely with magnifiers (science), we can notice that for the very first time George (usually very dominant) is behaving co-operatively with Alice.

Recording for assessment purposes is part of the process of education. Nevertheless, it is vital that we use profiles to record positive development. Isaacs (1930) always recommended a 'bottom-up' perspective of assessment which uses positive descriptions of cognitive competence in young children – that is, describing what children *can* do rather what they *cannot* do. Furthermore, 'we shouldn't allow assessment to drive the curriculum, rather [we should] use assessment to inform us of the children's needs and to help [us plan] differentiated activities' (Johnston, 1996, p. 89). Structuring and evaluating the way we monitor children's learning will not only inform our planning but also ensure more effective teaching.

Strategy	Advantages and disadvantages
• using recall at the end of the school day	• good, but not always reliable • good, but not usually an option
• taking notes just after a discussion with children	• can work if using sticky notes which will trigger recalled responses
• a colleague taking notes during a discussion	• reliable, but not always an option • can work with sticky notes as above
• using a tape recorder during discussion	• reliable, but requires children to be used to its 'presence' • takes time to listen through later to make notes

Figure 1: The advantages and disadvantages of four strategies for noting what children say.

About this book

In this introductory chapter I have tried to give the background to some of the principles held by the authors of this book. We are all aware of the pressures of teaching in a climate where the expectations of governments, parents and colleagues can be such that we lose sight of the way young children learn best. This book is an attempt to demonstrate best practice. The authors all have expertise and experience in two main areas: a subject discipline and early years education. They describe their experiences of teaching young children – showing how learning occurred across the curriculum in child-initiated play and in adult-directed activities.

The themes

The themes are chosen from areas of experience that are relevant and interesting to young children as well as reflecting that fascinating mixture of reality and fantasy that is the child's world. The themes include stories and nursery rhymes; families, and family gatherings and visits; early experiences of the living world; and how we co-operate and communicate with others. The themes are accounts of real situations, and the authors and their colleagues were working with children from a wide variety of backgrounds, including children with special educational needs and English as an additional language.

Key focus areas

These indicate subject areas such as 'language, science and mathematics' as well as generic skills and attitudes such as 'creativity, problem-solving and sharing ideas'. The reader will see that a considerable amount of learning occurred outside of these focus areas. But, by focusing our observations on these areas, it was possible to clarify our objectives, assess individual progress, and evaluate our provision for further learning.

Essential resources

This lists those resources used in the principal activities in the theme.

Planned outcomes

This defines the expectations we might have of many children in the group – in the development of attitudes, skills or knowledge.

Starting-points

These generally indicate the very first starting-point, whether initiated by the children or directed by the practitioners, such as reading *The Tiger Who Came To Tea* (Kerr, 1973). Subsequently, there may be many starting-points within a theme. Sometimes a productive question from an adult becomes the starting-point for a new kind of play (e.g. 'Can you think of an animal that has short legs at the front and long legs at the back?' page 63), or a child's recalled experience sets off another pursuit of knowledge. Whichever it is, a good starting-point sets the mind and imagination racing, in an atmosphere of 'I know what we can do ...! Let's do ...!'

Setting up the learning environment

Whatever the starting-point, the adult practitioner will look for potential opportunities for extending that learning. This usually means planning further directed activities, in other curricular areas, to give individuals and groups opportunities to develop their skills and knowledge. Planned activities require the selection and collection of resources, allocating time and sometimes additional adult support. 'Play' may be spontaneous, but providing a broad, balanced curriculum requires planning.

Productive questions

The text here identifies those questions which encouraged children to expand their play, challenge their thinking, and produce more positive outcomes – for example 'Will the big seeds grow into big plants?' (page 46). Generally, the questions are person-centred and open-ended, to encourage several children to respond and offer their solutions to problems.

Teacher-directed challenges

The wording is deliberate here. This section identifies the *opportunities* for practitioners to challenge children's learning in particular ways, whether problem-solving or exploring language related to the task or play. The 'Set challenges' describe the specific actions of the adults that generated more discussion and/or problem-solving: for example, 'Who can make the longest drainpipe?'

Child-initiated responses to the setting

This recalls the adult observations of the children's behaviour and/or what was said (also echoed elsewhere in each theme). These exemplify some of the comments that might be transferred to pupil profiles for assessment and/or evaluation of the activities, challenges or resources. This provides material for discussion with colleagues as well as parents.

Key vocabulary/ Using the language

Each theme offers the opportunity to develop new vocabulary as well as to reinforce more familiar words. This is important for all children, but perhaps particularly for children for whom English is an additional language. Alongside the key words (e.g. *long, longer, short, shorter*), the authors show how these words may be used in relevant contexts and

identify for the reader when certain key words may enrich the children's concepts in particular subject areas (e.g. *invitation, guest … journey, route, travel*).

The children's voices and teacher reflections

Throughout each theme, the reader will 'hear' the voices of the children. What the children say can be very revealing. Adults working with the children used these responses to reflect on the children's learning and on what was notable from the adults' point of view. Once again, such reflections might be transferred to pupil profiles or used for discussion with colleagues.

Further activities

This section expands upon the activities designed to extend the learning environment outlined at the beginning of each theme. We hope that these give enough detail for readers to try them out when the opportunity arises while the children are pursuing an interest similar to that of the theme. These activities will encourage development of skills and knowledge across the curriculum, from art to using an Intel microscope.

Assessment for learning

By now, there is considerable evidence of children's achievement. On this page, the learning is specifically related to the *Curriculum Guidance* (QCA, 2000) recommendations for pupil profiles and other formal records. The reader will see that observations by all the significant adults in the child's education are valued: parents, carers, teachers and auxiliary assistants.

References and further resources

This lists a wide range of resources – including books, both information and story books, ICT resources, equipment and materials – and where they can be obtained.

Photographs

Finally, but most importantly, throughout the book, we let the reader see and hear the children. As I said earlier, early years practitioners are adept at interpreting what is happening from a picture or a child's response. And pictures can inspire – prompting ideas and effective challenges for readers to use with children in their own setting. Above all, we wanted to let the children 'speak for themselves'. We hope we succeeded, and we hope you enjoy the book.

Max de Bóo

February 2004

Bibliography

Beetlestone, F. (1998) *Creative Children, Creative Teaching*. Buckingham: Open University Press.

Blenkin, G. V. and Kelly, A. V. (1992) *Assessment in Early Childhood Education*. London: Paul Chapman.

Boorman, P. and Rogers, M. (2000) 'Science through everyday activities' in de Bóo, M. (ed) *Laying the Foundations in the Early Years*. Hatfield: ASE, pp. 39-47.

Bruner, J. and Haste, H. (eds) (1993) *Making Sense: The child's construction of the world*. London: Methuen.

de Bóo, M. (1999) *Enquiring Children, Challenging Teaching*. Buckingham, Open University Press

de Bóo, M. (ed) (2000) *Laying the Foundations in the Early Years*. Hatfield: ASE.

Devon Curriculum Services (n.d.) *The Plays Pack: Purposeful learning activities for young scientists*. Exeter: Devon County Council.

Donaldson, M. (1987) *Children's Minds*. London: Fontana Press.

Feasey, R. (1999) *Primary Science and Literacy Links*. Hatfield: ASE.

Feasey, R. (2000) 'Children's language in science' in de Boo, M. (ed) Laying the Foundations in the Early Years. Hatfield: ASE, pp. 28-38.

Feasey, R. and Gallear, B. (2000) *Primary Science and Numeracy*. Hatfield: ASE.

Fisher, R. (1994) *Teaching Children to Think*. Hemel Hempstead: Simon and Schuster.

Frost, R. (1992) *The IT in Primary Science Book*. Hatfield: ASE.

Hutchin, V. (1999) *Tracking Significant Achievement in the Early Years*. London: Hodder and Stoughton.

Isaacs, S. (1930) *Intellectual Growth in Young Children*. London: Routledge and Kegan Paul.

Johnston, J. (1996) *Early Explorations in Science*. Buckingham: Open University Press.

Kerr, J. (1973) *The Tiger Who Came to Tea*. London: Collins Picture Lions.

Lobman, C. L. (2003) 'What should we create today? Improvisational teaching in play-based classrooms', *Early Years*, 23, 2.

Melhuish, E. C. and Moss, P. (eds) (1990) *Day-care for Young Children: International perspectives*. London: Routledge.

Merry, R. (1998) *Successful Children, Successful Teaching*. Buckingham: Open University Press.

Moyles, J. R. (1996) *Just Playing? The role and status of play in early childhood Education*. Buckingham: Open University Press.

Qualifications and Curriculum Authority (QCA) (2000) *Curriculum Guidance for the Foundation Stage*. London: QCA/DfEE.

Scottish Consultative Council on the Curriculum (1998) *Promoting Learning: Assessing children's progress 3 to 5*. Edinburgh: The Scottish Office.

Selley, N. (1999) *The Art of Constructivist Teaching in the Primary School*. London: David Fulton Publishers.

Siraj-Blatchford, J. and MacLeod-Brudenell, I. (1999) *Supporting Science, Design and Technology in the Early Years*. Buckingham: Open University Press.

Vygotsky, L. (1978) *Mind in Society: The development of higher psychological processes*. Cambridge MA: Harvard University Press.

Vygotsky, L. (1986) *Thought and Language*. Massachusetts Institute of Technology NY: Wiley.

Wood, D. (1992) *How Children Think and Learn*. Oxford: Blackwell Publishers.

theme: problem-solving in the water

save incy wincy spider

This theme takes a favourite nursery rhyme with children and uses it as the starting-point for a series of problem-solving activities in the water tray.

The nursery rhyme

Incy Wincy Spider climbed up the water spout.
Down came the rain and washed the spider out.
Out came the sun shine and dried up all the rain.
So Incy Wincy Spider climbed up the spout again!

Before you start …

Key focus areas

The key focus areas are:
- Science
- Language
- Construction
- Spatial awareness
- Problem-solving
- Sharing ideas

Essential resources
- The nursery rhyme
- Water tray
- Different lengths and sizes of drain pipes
- Connecting collars for pipes
- Plastic spider (or spiders)
- Watering can
- Plastic bottles
- Pieces of guttering of different sizes

Planned outcomes

Children should be able to:
- use the piping to build a drainpipe for Incy
- work collaboratively and share the equipment and take turns
- problem-solve – for example, to try different pipes if one set does not fit together.

Setting up the learning environment

Provide the following materials in the water tray: plastic piping (e.g. drainpipes), pieces of guttering and connecting brackets, a plastic spider and a watering can.

Starting-points

Spiders

Teach children the rhyme, explain that 'water spout' in this context means 'drainpipe', and then engage children in exploratory talk about spiders. This might be accompanied by, for example:

- model or puppet spiders that have the correct number of legs (eight) and two parts to the body
- live spiders kept in a transparent container
- using the interactive whiteboard to show children a close-up view of a spider using an Intel Computer Microscope.

Our starting-point

We taught the children the Incy Wincy spider nursery rhyme. Although some of them were already familiar with it, we wanted all of the children to be able to repeat it independently of an adult.

It was very easy to create a drainpipe: we bought pieces of piping from a local builders' merchant, cut them down, and made sure that the edges were safe.

These were placed in the water tray along with a large plastic spider, big enough so that it could be dropped into the drainpipe and appear at the other end. There was also a watering can to simulate rain, and to wash Incy down the pipe into the water tray.

When the children were familiar with the story in the nursery rhyme and had explored the different things in the water tray, we changed the story so that something different happened.

'One day Incy Wincy Spider climbed up the spout [the word 'drainpipe' could be substituted], just as he always did – and as he climbed inside, guess what?'

It looks scary!

It's got one, two, three, four, five, six, seven, eight ... it's got eight legs.

My Dad picks spiders up in his hand, my Mum doesn't like them.

Look, it's got hairs on its legs.

We encouraged suggestions from children, by asking them what they thought happened next. When children offered interesting ideas they were taken on board, but when children needed prompting we continued and said:

'Oh no! What do you know! Incy Wincy Spider got stuck. Yes, stuck right in the middle of the drainpipe.'

We talked with the children, asking them questions such as:

- Why do you think Incy Wincy Spider got stuck?
- Do you think Incy had been eating too many insects, and got too fat?
- Was there something else in the drainpipe that meant Incy Wincy Spider could not get past?
- What could it be?
- How could we get Incy out of the drainpipe without hurting it?

Productive questions

- Where have you seen spiders?
- What do you think spiders eat?
- How do you think Incy gets back up the drainpipe?
- What do you think happens to all the water when the sun comes out?
- Where does all the water go?
- What makes you think that?
- Where have you seen really big spiders?
- Have you seen a spider's web?
- What did it look like?
- Have you held a tarantula?
- What did it feel like?
- Where do you think we could find out more about spiders?

Challenges and responses

Having learned the nursery rhyme, children recognised the different pieces in the water tray, and had the freedom to explore the different pieces of piping to find out:

- how the different pieces fitted together
- different ways in which they could make Incy travel through the pipe (fast, slow)
- how to make long drainpipes.

Children joined in 'show and tell', explaining what they did in the water tray to other children. We asked them questions about what they did, to encourage children to talk about cause and effect, how they put things together, and how they solved problems.

Teacher-directed challenges

This setting provided opportunities for teacher-directed challenges focusing on:

- Problem-solving: finding different ways to get Incy out of the drainpipe
- Development of spatial awareness and associated language, e.g. *inside, outside, down, up*
- Working together by sharing ideas and helping each other – for example, one child holding the drainpipe, the other pouring water down the pipe, and then alternating roles
- The development of exploratory language

related to the task, such as *push, pour, drown, drainpipe, next, again, try this, do that, more water*.

Set challenges

As children worked with increasing confidence in the water tray, we intervened with further challenges by offering additional problems – for example:

- Change the drainpipe so that Incy Wincy does not drown.
- Who can make the longest drainpipe?
- How will you keep the pieces together?
- How can you make a drainpipe that does not let Incy Wincy Spider fall straight down into the water?

Child-initiated responses to the setting

In this setting most children were very excited about the new things in the water tray and were eager to have their turn. They constantly repeated putting the spider down the drainpipe and were always delighted when it got stuck!

It was interesting to see several children place the drainpipe in the guttering and use the watering can to pour water onto the drainpipe so that it was pushed down the guttering.

Some of the children connected the different parts of the drainpipe together, others watched and then copied.

Tahmina did not engage with the materials in the water tray, but stood to one

side. While watching the other children she sang the 'Incy Wincy spider' rhyme quietly to herself.

Language

Key vocabulary

spout drainpipe pieces connectors long short longer spider climb legs body head lives crawls rain water watering can hard drops sun out clouds dry hot shine water poured fast slow wet

Encouraging children to use the language

'**Down** came the rain.'
'**Up** climbed the spider.'
'**Out** came the sun.'

Language across the curriculum

Mathematics – positional language
up   down   below
side   on top   underneath

Children's voices

Abdul: [walks the spider along the guttering saying] 'Spider. It's stuck.'

Teacher: 'What could you do to get it out?'

Abdul: 'Like this' [puts hand in the tube and pushes the spider out]

Teacher: 'Shall we see if we can get him out with water?'

Sabbi: 'Yes.'

[They pour water in the tube and the spider comes out.]

Abdul: 'It's a magic trick!' [Puts spider in the long pipe, then exclaims] 'Wow it's stuck!'

Sabbi: 'I'm pour it. I'm pour the water.'

[Abdul takes the spider out by hand.]

Teacher: 'How did you get spider out?'

Abdul:

আমি আত হাবাইয়া আনিলিাছ

(I brought it out with my hand.)

Sabbi: 'He put it in there,' [pointing to the tube] 'I'm pour the water.' [As she watches the water trickling down, her facial expression was animated.]

Teacher: 'What is it?'

Sabbi: 'It's a waterfall going down.'

Abdul: [Puts the spider back in the tube, and watches as Sabbi pouring water in the small tube then looks at the teacher]

অবঠিদি আইস্া ওবঠিদি যস্দি

(Look, it comes this way then goes this way) [showing the direction of the flow with his finger].

Teacher reflections

'These two children do not often work together, so I was surprised to find that their level of co-operation was high. On reflection this was because it is hard to play with the spider and hold the drainpipe vertical at the same time, which meant that they had to co-operate for it to work. It had not occurred to me before that the type of task and materials placed in the tray could make these demands. In future I will try to ensure that I make equipment and activities available that demand this level of co-operation from children.

'It was interesting to not the use of "I'm" rather than "I am", and "I'm pour" rather than "I'm pouring it" suggesting that some scaffolding needs to take place to help the children develop the language relating to talking about themselves and what they are doing.

'We were surprised to hear Sabbi relate the effect of pouring water from the watering can to a waterfall.

'Children do not always respond verbally to adult questions or suggestions, more often they respond by doing something specific.'

Further activities

Extending the learning environment

- Story bags with the nursery rhyme and artefacts
- Displays about spiders
- Large spider's web as a display that includes questions and vocabulary linked to the nursery rhyme and spiders
- Art area where children can sponge-print spiders
- Picture books about spiders
- Tinkering table where children can explore things such as plastic jumping spiders
- Construction area where children can make spiders using different construction materials.

Open guttering

Place open guttering in the water tray to contrast its use with (closed) drainpipes.

Children could be offered the plastic spider and other objects (for example, very large marbles), which they can send down the guttering so that they can watch the movement of the objects and of the water.

Children might race objects down the guttering, move the guttering up and down to see what happens, and even use the guttering as a scoop.

Wind-up toys

A range of wind-up animals such as frogs, spiders and whales are placed in the water tray with large pipes. Children are asked, before they go into the tray, to find ways of getting the wind-up animals through the pipes (or tunnels).

Huge spiders

With adult support, children use an Intel computer microscope to view a spider (a dead spider is easiest) either on an interactive whiteboard or on a computer screen. Through effective questioning, the adult helps the children to focus on key features of the spider. For example:

- How many legs does it have?
- Where are the eyes?
- How many are there?
- What are the legs like?
- Where do you think the mouth is?
- What does it look like?

Pop-up book page

Make a pop-up book page with the children. Use flexible card to create the drainpipe, and stick a picture of a spider on a length of card, the end of which is a pull tab.

Children can then pull and push the tab so that Incy Wincy Spider is pushed and pulled up and down the drainpipe.

Observing spiders

With adult support, children view a live spider kept in a transparent tank. The adult asks a range of questions, such as:

- What is the spider doing?
- How does it walk?
- Where does it sit most of the time?
- What colours can you see on the spider?
- Why is a spider that colour/those colours?

Observational sponge-prints

Once they are familiar with the shape of spiders, how many legs they have, and the position of their body parts, offer children pieces of sponge that are cut into suitable shapes to enable them to create sponge-

prints of spiders. Challenge children to:

- use appropriate shapes for different parts of the body
- place each body part in the correct position
- put detail on the body.

Allow children to refer to pictures, computer photographs, etc.

School drainpipes and guttering

Walk around the school buildings and look for drainpipes - especially when it's raining! How many are there? Where are they? What's happening? Where does the rain come from? Where does it go? Leaky pipes or gutters can be a good source of discussion. Why do they need to be fixed? Who will do it? Can we tell someone who will fix it?

Rain music (creative development)

Challenge the children to make the sound of the rain using their bodies and/or using instruments? Provide opportunities for children to experiment with sounds, rhythmic patterns and tempo and record sounds made.

Aims

- Build and construct with a wide range of objects.
- Show curiosity, observe and manipulate objects.

Teacher comments

Sabbi was able to use the pipes to construct a drainpipe for Incy Wincy. She overcame problems through trial and error, learning from each experience how to connect different lengths of drainpipe to make one long drainpipe.

She persevered, and showed curiosity in wanting to know why the end-piece was curved.

Assessment for learning

We should look at assessment from the point of view of what it can do to enhance the experience of learning science (De Bóo, 2000, p. 48). In science the teacher needs to access children's thinking by challenging them to:

- explain what they are doing
- suggest the reason for doing something
- make connections – for example, cause and effect
- share ideas.

Opportunities should be taken to assess other areas (where appropriate) of early years development such as language and personal, social and emotional development.

References and further resources

Carle, E. (1995) *The Very Lonely Firefly*. Hamish Hamilton Children's Books.

Carle, E. (2000) *The Bad-Tempered Ladybird*. Picture Puffins.

Carle, E. (2002) *The Very Hungry Caterpillar*. Picture Puffins.

Foster, J. and Thompson, C. (1996) *First Verses: Finger rhymes*. Oxford University Press.

Gribbin, M. and Bull, P. (1995) *Big Ocean Creatures*. Ladybird Books.

Gribbin, M. and Tewson, A. (1996) *Big Bugs!* Ladybird First Discovery Books.

Hale, J. and Novick, M. (2003) *Double Delights: Nursery rhymes*. Southwood Books.

Milne, A.A. and Shepard, E.H. (1989) *'Forgiven'* (about a lost beetle) in *Now We Are Six*. Methuen Young Books.

Morris, J. (1993) *The Animal Roundabout*. Dorling Kindersley.

Pluckrose, H. and Fairclough, C. (1992) *Thinkabout Floating and Sinking*. Watts.

Poole, S. (1994) *Minibeasts Photo Pack*. Folens.

Aims

- Examine living things to find out more about them.
- Find out about living things and identify some features of living things.

Auxiliary comments

Abdul was excited when observing the spider using the Intel Microscope. He talked independently about where he had seen spiders in his house, and that his dad was afraid of them (he thought this was funny). He was able to suggest body parts (e.g. legs, body, head), and when prompted talked about his own body parts and the spider's.

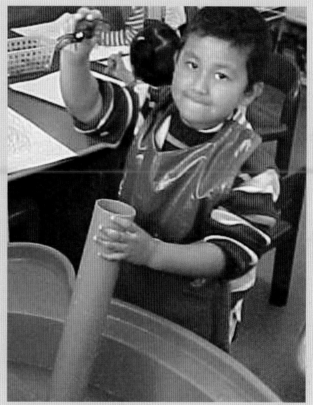

Aims

- Talk about what is seen and what is happening.
- Explore objects, show an interest in why things happen and how things work.

Parent comment

James chatted all the way home about Incy Wincy Spider and making the drainpipe. He also talked about seeing the spider on the board, and how spiders make their webs. I was surprised how much he knew and how excited he was. He went and collected spiders from outside in the garden when he got home, to take to school the next day.

theme: role play and language

do I have to wear my coat?

There is no more useful a resource for capturing children's imagination than a good picture book. In this theme Tatty Ratty was used as a stimulus for cross-curricular activities.

Before you start ...

Key focus areas
The key focus areas are:
- Communication, language and literacy – talk for thinking
- Knowledge and understanding of the world – a sense of time and place
- Creativity
- Personal, social and emotional
- Sharing ideas

Essential resources
- A copy of the picture book *Tatty Ratty* by Helen Cooper (2002)
- A soft toy (preferably a rabbit) with sets of clothes to match those provided for the children.

Dressing-up clothes such as: gloves, scarves, rain coats and hats, sun hats, sunglasses, beach bags, pirate and astronaut costumes, bed covers, spades, back-packs

Simple props such as: bear masks, blankets, beach towels, buckets, back-packs, drink flasks, lunch-boxes, umbrellas, porridge bowls and spoons

Setting up the learning environment
- Use these resources and props to set up a number of areas, including ones for role play, table-top play, a model-making and construction table, a writing table and a book corner.
- Set up the role-play area as a Travelling Theatre. Stock it with props and clothes suitable for different climates and locations. Include props that will encourage the children to use their imagination and to take Tatty Ratty to somewhere new or to another story.

From Tatty Ratty by Helen Cooper; published by Doubleday/Corgi. Reprinted by permission of The Random House Group Ltd.

Planned outcomes
Children should be able to:
- use spoken language appropriately when in role
- negotiate and adapt their ideas through working with others
- use what they have learned and their own experiences in their play.

Tatty Ratty
Tatty Ratty by Helen Cooper (2002) is a very clever book. It tells two parallel stories about a little girl, Molly, who loses her toy rabbit, Tatty Ratty, and who imagines what is happening to him as she carries on with her everyday life. For example, while Molly is at breakfast, he is eating the Three Bears' porridge; as she plays with a boat in the bath, Tatty Ratty is on a pirate ship. The book is an ideal stimulus for promoting learning in all areas of the foundation curriculum and was used here to make links with the national curriculum.

"Can I drive the bus soon?"

"I've forgotten my packed lunch!"

"There's a good view from the window."

"He's a good driver."

Starting-points

We were very concerned to provide a learning environment and activities that would allow children to make links between the different areas of the early years curriculum, working on the theory that children learn best when they build on previous knowledge and experience. The obvious starting-point for this scheme of work was the book itself.

Our starting-point

We read *Tatty Ratty* to the children until they became very familiar with it. Fortunately, we had found a toy rabbit that was very like the one in the book and that soon became Tatty Ratty to the children. It did not take long before he became so loved that the children wanted to include him in everything they did.

The book is a series of adventures, so we decided, with the children's help, to change our role-play area into a Travelling Theatre. We aimed to give the children the freedom to use the resources we had put in it to work out their own play situations. We were particularly interested in:

- Looking for opportunities to see children setting their play in some of the places we had found out about together
- Giving children opportunities to practise different kinds of spoken language
- Seeing the extent to which children were able to integrate what they had learned from direct teaching and child-directed activities into their play.

One cold Monday morning, after it had been snowing, a group set up rows of chairs, something they did without much discussion. They had obviously done this before. They then went to the Theatre, selected woolly hats, gloves and scarves and dressed Tatty Ratty in his warm jacket. One boy then elected himself as coach driver. An adult asked, 'Where are you going?' One of the more dominant girls replied, 'We're going to the ski lift'. The children then spent about ten minutes going on a coach journey, swaying together as the coach went round bends, and talking, without adult intervention, about the windy road and slippery surface. The driver led this part of the play, calling 'Watch out!' as he approached an imaginary bend.

However, it was the girls who were more involved in the conversation and who gave a voice to Tatty Ratty. When asked 'How long will it take to get there?', a child replied 'We're there!' and the chairs became the lift. 'What's the weather like?', they were asked. 'It's freezing!', a child called back, and the group began to huddle together and shiver.

At this point one of the boys said 'My mum's gone to Spain today'. Someone said, 'Let's go there now' – and, without hesitation, all the children returned to the dressing-up box to put on sun hats and sunglasses, gave Tatty Ratty a straw hat and a cotton shirt, and off they went, once more travelling by coach.

Challenges and responses

Teacher-directed challenges

This setting provided opportunities for teacher-directed challenges focusing on:

- Extending the range of subject-specific vocabulary by modelling it for the children
- Developing problem-solving: 'what would we wear if we went to …?'
- Encouraging collaborative play for those children who found it difficult
- Intervening sensitively in the children's play to move their thinking on – e.g. 'I've forgotten my hat. How can I keep my ears warm?'

Set challenges

For those children who have grasped the concepts in the role play, extend their play by providing materials that help them to develop it – for example:

- Provide holiday brochures so that the children can choose where Tatty Ratty will go next.
- Telling them Tatty Ratty has won a holiday – and asking the children to pack his suitcase.
- Ask the children to make Tatty Ratty a rain hat.

Child-initiated responses to the setting

After looking at the inside of a cuckoo-clock, two boys made their own clock mechanism from plastic cogs. We subsequently produced a display of clock mechanisms.

The children switched to playing out their own holiday experiences of going to the beach. One girl, in a very adult voice, said 'It's getting late. I'm going to change for dinner'. She then 'walked back to the hotel' and put on a pretty skirt for the evening. This was what she was used to doing on holiday.

Another child, working in a different area of the room, was repeatedly returning to the book. He was matching the pictures in the book to the story board that we had made in the book corner.

Further challenges

Where to go next with role play:

- Introduce a new character to the play, an adult acting in role. For example, the adult may say 'Stop the coach – snow is blocking the road'. Decide as a group what to do next, what equipment you will need, who will go for help, what the dangers are, etc.
- Tatty Ratty has just heard that Molly is missing him. What is the quickest way for him to get home?

We looked at two Swiss Cuckoo Clocks.
We tasted Swiss chocolate.

Switzerland

Look at the mountains
Can you see the skiers?

Lauren's mummy has seen the ice palace.

is cold d. We made our own ice sculpture.

What clothes will we have to wear in that country?

What is the weather like?

Tatty Ratty loved the journey to Switzerland on the plane.
He wore warm clothes to go up in a ski lift.

Weather C

Scotland

Children's voices

Harriet: 'We're going to the ski-lift.'

Sophie: 'Hurry up and get on the coach!'

Harriet: 'Make sure we don't forget Tatty Ratty.'

George: 'I'm going to be driver. Hang on! It's very slippery.'

Harriet: 'It's very cold in Switzerland.'

George: 'And there are lots of mountains.'

Harriet: 'My Mum went to Switzerland, and she went skiing.'

George: 'Bet she fell over.'

Harriet: 'Yeah … and she hurt her bottom!'

Teacher reflections

'It was so pleasing to observe the extent to which the children were able to fuse their individual experiences and their imagination. They took things from their everyday life, the lessons they had been learning with me, and a toy rabbit that had fired their imagination. What was amazing was their skill at weaving all this together, in play that they obviously found so fulfilling. Watching and listening, I was reminded how easy it is to underestimate children's intellectual ability and how important talk is in helping all that to happen.

'I am sure that there were several contributing factors to the success of this piece of play. It happened towards the end of term, so the children had lots of learning experiences to draw on. Secondly, the degree of collaboration within the group was very strong: they worked as a unit. The girls initiated the activity but they did not tell the boys what to do. They guided events through conversation.

'My big question is: Where do I take the learning from here? This group is obviously at the point where they need a new challenge. How do I help them to extend their spoken language? Perhaps I could ask them to 'tell the story' of their play to a larger group of children. The need to explain and describe would require them to use a different speech genre and different vocabulary.

'There is a need also to provide more adult-led problem solving activities.'

Language

Key vocabulary

journey	holiday	visit
winter	summer	freezing
cold	hot	lost
found	postcard	stamp
holiday	cog	wheel
went	going	came
with	story	real
up	down	in
out	along	by
country	mountain	sea
steep	slippery	slide
snow	very	Tatty Ratty
author	book	coach
Switzerland	ski	ski-lift
cuckoo-clock	pirates	spaceship

Encouraging children to use the language appropriately to:

- re-tell a story
- play in role
- read or repeat familiar phrases from the book
- communicate in writing at their own level

Language across the curriculum

Geography

home	go by coach

country	mountain	seaside

far away	go on a journey

History

old   yesterday   last time

Technology

wheel	cog	join

Mathematics – positional language

up   down   below

side   on top   underneath

Further activities

Take a toy home

- Have a teddy or toy rabbit that the children can take turns to take home for the weekend. Provide it with a notebook or diary page so that the child and their family can write simple accounts, draw pictures and even take photographs of the toy's adventures. These can then be shared with the other children afterwards.

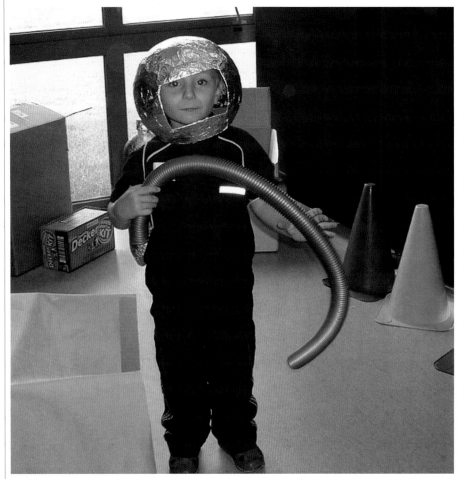

Postcard home

- Send a postcard to the class from Tatty Ratty. With adult support, the children send one to Tatty Ratty in return. Place blank cards in the role play or writing/mark-making area for the children to use. Don't forget to put stamps there too!

Indoor/outdoor play

- Have large blocks, planks and cardboard boxes available. Encourage children to build a vehicle from the story, e.g. a bus, a pirate ship, a spaceship.

- Make the bus station where Tatty Ratty is lost. Make a lost-property office. Include posters, telephones, notebooks, a list of lost toys, etc.

Make a big book

- Encourage children to make a collage illustration of a scene from one of the stories used in the book. Ensure that there is a selection of materials and media available for the children to use. When the illustrations are complete, ask the children to re-tell the story; act as scribe. Make the pages into a big book that you can read with them.

Construction toys and maps

- Build a railway for the Three Bears' journey, e.g. with Brio. Have small toys, e.g. Compare Bears, and a small Tatty Ratty to take on a train ride.
- With adult help, the more able children can place the track on a large piece of paper and draw round it to make a simple map.

Looking at materials

- Investigate materials for keeping warm or at clothes suitable for different weather conditions. The children could dress Tatty Ratty or a teddy bear for each type of weather.
- Make a raincoat for Tatty Ratty. Which materials will we use? The raincoat the material needs to be waterproof. Children could be introduced to the idea of waterproof. Try raincoats on outside and create a shower using a sprinkler. Then try different materials in school using a watering can and test very different materials such as plastic, cotton and net.

Assessment for learning

The kind of role play that we have been considering is a very rich source of evidence for assessment. The main aims of the activity were to encourage children to use what they had learned and to develop their facility with spoken language. The assessment of the children's talk should not be limited to the complexity of the vocabulary or language-structures that they use, although this should be included. Rather, it is a method of assessing what children know and understand, and their ability to think and solve problems. Although it was possible to make assessments about many areas of learning, here we will concentrate on Communication, Language and Literacy, noting what children can do and where their learning might next be extended. The criteria used are adapted from the English statutory Foundation Stage Profile.

References and further resources

Burningham, J. (2001) *Mr Gumpy's Outing*. Red Fox.

Curry, P. (1990) *The Big Red Bus Ride*. Picture Lions.

Henderson, K. (1995) *The Little Boat*. Walker Books.

Hughes, S. (1998) *Out and About* (poems). Walker Books.

Hutchins, P. (1993) *The Wind Blew*. Atheneum.

Lister, D. (1996) 'Hats' in Foster, J. and Thompson, C. (ed) *First Verses: Finger rhymes*. Oxford University Press.

MacDonald, A. and Fox-Davies, S. (1993) *Little Beaver and The Echo*. Walker Books.

McKee, D. (1990) *Elmer (The story of a patchwork elephant)*. Red Fox Picture Books.

Oxfam staff (1996) *Photo Opportunities: Activities for the primary classroom* (photos from around the world). Oxfam and ASE.

Roffey, M. (1994) *How Do We Get There?* Macmillan Children's Books.

Rosen, M. and Oxenbury, H. (2003) *We're Going on a Bear Hunt*. Walker Books.

Aims

- Negotiating with others, taking account of what they say.

Teacher comments

At the point in their play where they were in 'Spain', Anna and Chloe both wanted to wear the same skirt. Anna said, 'I'll have it this time and then we can swap.' 'All right then,' replied Chloe, 'but I'll have the beads.' Between them they had defused a situation that might have led to disagreement.

Aims

- Use talk to organise events.

Teacher comments

This group of children took on speech roles in the organisation of their play. As they were putting the chairs out, Shaun said 'We won't get all of them in.' 'Yeah we will, we've all got one', replied Tom. 'Tatty's got to have a chair', said Jenny. The children carried on sorting the chairs until they had them exactly where they wanted them, with a seat in front for the driver.

You could extend the children's learning by playing barrier games where one child has to tell another how to recreate a pattern by using precise vocabulary.

Aims

- Continue to be interested, excited and motivated to learn (PSE).
- Retell narratives in the correct sequence, drawing on language patterns in the stories.

Parent comment

Tatty Ratty became part of our family. Every day, on the way home from school, Lucy told me about what they had been doing in class. She told me about the things they had made Tatty Ratty do. I was really surprised at how much she talked about the story and how enthusiastic she was. We've got the usual collection of fairy stories, The Three Bears and so on; Lucy hunted them out so that she could tell me which of the stories Tatty Ratty had been in. I was pleased because she usually doesn't talk much about school.

Tatty Ratty went to have breakfast with the three bears

He went to see the moon

theme: learning to share

it's my turn!

This theme takes a group discussion and uses it as the starting-point for a series of mathematical activities based on games and other toys.

Before you start ...

Key focus areas
The key focus areas are:
- Mathematics (number, shape and space)
- Personal, social and emotional development
- Information and communications technology
- Physical education
- Sharing ideas

Essential resources
- Dice with dots, word and number (use sticky labels over a standard 1–6 die if blank dice are not available)
- Counters or other winning tokens
- Selection of other dice or spinners for the children's own games
- Unifix or other interlocking cubes
- Copies of the blank tracks for the further challenge on page 35.

I only need one more.

This is boring – let's use a different dice and get to a million.

Oh-oh, I got all twos!

Please can I go first this time because then I'll win.

Planned outcomes
Children should be able to:
- play a two-person game involving numbers up to ten, and understand taking turns.
- talk about their game, and understand fairness and the criteria for winning.
- begin to use ordinal language accurately.

Setting up the learning environment
- Make a display of toys or photographs of toys, from the present and the past, including mechanical toys which can be the focus of a 'how do they work?' discussion.
- Have a game playing table set up that includes Unifix cubes, counters, dice and spinners and blank pieces of track (see page 35).
- Provide books and rhymes that introduce the idea of a repeating pattern or order, such as *The Enormous Turnip* (Slier, 1998).
- Use a special token to signify whose turn it is to talk in 'circle time' or 'show and tell' sessions.
- Select an indoor or outdoor play area in which the children can use skipping ropes and/or games such as the hand-pyramid game (alternate hands in pile, take turns to remove hand from bottom and place on top).

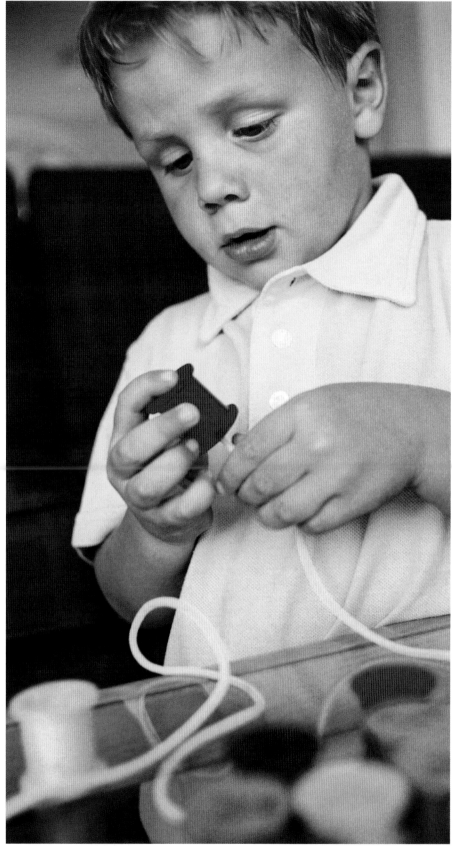

Starting-points

Children interact with others in a turn-taking way in many different activities, formal and informal. This theme uses formal game playing to reinforce the idea of turns, and to provide an opportunity for children to experiment in making up their own games.

Our starting-point

Using a collection of games and toys, we initiated a discussion of who would play with them, where, how, similarities and differences, etc. In particular we focused on which games were good to play alone and which need other people, and in the latter case how many people.

Next, we talked about playing fairly and taking turns. We introduced a simple game involving two teams. We split the children up into two groups, and they took turns to throw a large die with 1 on three faces and 2 on the other three faces (shown as number, word and spots). The teams took the corresponding number of Unifix cubes and put them together to make a tower. The winning team was the first to get to ten cubes in their tower.

We continued the discussion about taking turns, we photocopied the register list and used it as a focus for questioning or taking turns. We also talked about fairness, winning and losing, and what made a game a good one.

We then set up the table so that pairs of children could play the same game. We then introduced resources that enabled them to make up their own game using either dice and counters or cubes, or track.

We provided extra support for children not confident with numbers up to ten by collecting won items into a limited space – e.g. filling ten holes on a peg board, or threading buttons, beads or bobbins onto a limited length of string; or by matching sizes – e.g. making a tower of Unifix the same height as another.

Productive questions

- What games do you play at home?
- Who do you play with?
- Which is your favourite toy/game?
- Why is it a favourite?
- Do you watch games (or sports) on television, or go to watch games?
- Do you watch or play any team games? How many play on each side? How do you win?
- Taking turns in the classroom – how do we choose who has the next turn?
- Taking turns at home – what do you need to take turns in doing? How do you decide?
- What are the good things about taking turns?
- What are the not so good things about taking turns?

Challenges and responses

Teacher-directed challenges

This setting provided opportunities for teacher-directed challenges focusing on:

- ordinal language: *first, second, next, last*
- comparative language to decide the winner: *more, less*
- the idea of alternate turns for two people
- good game criteria: *fairness, luck, win, lose*

Set challenges

As the children became more and more engaged in their games, we suggested further challenges, offering additional problems and resources, for example:

- Make up a different game using blank dice and bigger numbers.
- Make up a track game using dice and a prepared board (or they can make up their own board).
- Make up a game for more than two people. Record the rules (with support) for others to play the game.

Child-initiated responses to the setting

- Even playing the simple initial game requires the children to work on several concepts simultaneously. Some needed support to remember whose turn it was and to count out the number of won objects.
- Other children played independently immediately, and were soon eager to alter games to them more interesting. They made the winning number bigger and then realised that this did not affect the game, just how long it took!
- Two children were not satisfied with the offered game and wanted to change it straight away. They wanted to know if they could play with three people, so the teacher joined in. They thought this was more exciting. It also generated much comparative language as they kept an eye on each other's won collections.

Further challenges

The children were shown several track-board games and then encouraged to work with a partner to design a game on a blank track. They then shared this with the rest of the class, and the teacher mediated the discussion to:

- discuss the rules of the game, what constituted a win, and the idea of fairness,
- use number words correctly, and
- encourage ordinal and comparative language.

Language
Key vocabulary

(number words up to ten – cardinal and ordinal)

game dice spinner turn fair last next more less fewer plus faster slower taller one more add-on difference luck win lose

Encouraging children to use the language
Mathematical language
cardinal numbers: **one** to **ten**
ordinal numbers: **first** to **tenth**
comparative: **more, less, fewer, plus, shorter, taller**

Talking about turn-taking
Talking about turn-taking can be extended by:

- drawing attention to order and turn-taking in other classroom activities
- reciting rhymes that involve ordinal as well as cardinal numbers
- setting up computers with two-person games for the children to access freely.

Language across the curriculum
Language for negotiating – please, your/my turn, thank you, etc.

Children's voices

Robert: 'It's a race, it's a race …'

Cally: 'A two! I'm winning … I've won.'

Robert: '… but that's not fair. I haven't gone the right times.'

Cally: 'Yes, I got there first.'

Robert: 'But … but … we didn't do the same.'

Cally: 'Yes we did. I went, then you went.'

Robert: 'But that isn't right because I have to go one time or … or … see … how many times should we do it? I have to do it again.'

Cally: 'No, then you'll win.'

Robert: 'I'm going to tell – it's not fair … Mrs M!'

Teacher reflections

'This conversation took place over a period of time while the children were playing and then inventing their own track game. The track provided was blank with ten spaces, a start and a finish. The game was exactly the same as the initial one we had introduced – first to ten – but using movement along the track rather than collecting buttons.

'This was the first time any of the children recognised the advantage of going first. Robert realised this very soon and wanted to rectify it. Cally's reluctance was not only because she didn't want to lose, but also because she hadn't gained the same insight.

'Their conversation led on to a whole-class discussion about going first and making sure everyone had the same number of goes. We left this problem for the children to solve themselves. Most relied on memory. One pair had a token which stayed with the person who went first.

'Making up a game which works requires a far more sophisticated degree of thinking than merely playing the game. Adult surveillance was essential to ensure there were no emotional disasters!'

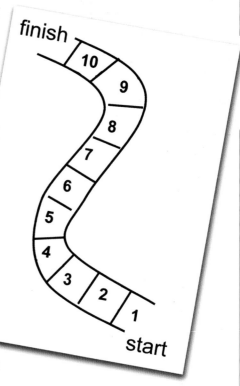

Further activities

One potato

<blockquote>
One potato, two potatoes,
Three potatoes, four,
Five potatoes, six potatoes,
Seven potatoes, more.
</blockquote>

Teach the rhyme and the rules for playing 'one potato' to a small group of children. They stand in a circle and put out both fists. The caller stands in the middle and touches each fist in turn along with the rhyme; whichever fist is touched on 'more' is put behind its owner's back and is not used again in the game. The winner is the one who has their fist left in the game at the end. This can become quite addictive, as the children teach each other to play it.

As an extended challenge you could ask the children to predict who will win. Some

mathematically very able children will puzzle over this for some time and deduce their own rules for winning.

My team

Towards the end of the topic, extend it to include a survey of the children's favourite team games, or toys, or board games, and make a display to illustrate the results.

'Ten happy clowns'

This clown rhyme (from Atkinson *et al.,* 1997) uses ordinal language. Teach it to the children and encourage them to act out the actions in order. They could practise it and perform it to an audience.

<blockquote>
Ten happy clowns
Were standing in a row.
The first said 'Good day'
And the second bowed low.
The third clapped his hands
And the fourth turned around.
The fifth stamped his feet
And the sixth touched the ground.
The seventh gave a hop
And the eighth jumped so high.
The ninth gave a wave
And the tenth said 'goodbye'.
</blockquote>

The children could then make up a similar set of actions, although it is unlikely that they will make up a series which rhymes.

As a follow-up a pictorial zig-zag book can be made as a lasting record of the activity.

Grabbit!!

Children play in pairs. They have a pile of counters (or conkers or buttons) and take turns to 'grab' just *one*. The winner is the player who 'grabs' the last item.

The game can be made more exciting if the children take turns to say how many they

should take next time. You may have to adjust what is meant by winning in this case – perhaps the last player to successfully take the requisite number. The better the children are at estimating, the more likely they are to win.

Sequences

'Taking turns' moves nicely into the idea of repeating sequences. Use potato prints, or threading beads, or sticky shapes, to encourage the children to produce repeating patterns which they then describe to the rest of the group. Children needing more support may be helped by having a pattern to copy, or continue, rather than being given a free choice.

The washing line

Set up a line across the classroom with pictures pegged onto it. Rearrange the order each day and use the line as a starter for questions: what is the first picture? – the last? – the second? and so on. Or you could use paper plates on which the children draw their own faces and write their names.

Aims
- Use developing mathematical ideas and methods to solve practical problems.

Teacher comments
Leo took the initial track and coloured in special squares which were 'bombs'. If the counter landed on one of them it was 'blown up', and that was the end of the game for that player. He adjusted the number of bombs after one round (which was very short!), and changed the rules to make the penalty one of starting again instead of being out of the game. This was a fascinating example of analysis and evaluation.

Aims
- Interact with others, negotiating plans and taking turns in conversation.

Auxiliary comments
Having made turn-taking the focus during this period (of a few weeks), it was interesting to notice how often the children themselves found opportunities to point out turn-taking in informal activities. This was noticeable in the playground as well as in the classroom.

Aims
- Count reliably up to ten.
- Say and use number names in order in familiar contexts.

Parent comments
Adam was very taken with the whole idea of competitive games and was keen to explore all the ones we already had. There were several (e.g. Ludo) which I thought were going to be too complicated for him, but the amount of counting and checking that he insisted we did convinced me that playing games is one way I can support him in his understanding of numbers.

Assessment for learning

This activity primarily provides opportunities for children to explore the ideas of winning and losing and taking turns, all of which are an essential part of forming good relationships with their peers. There are also many opportunities for assessing the children on their understanding of early numbers. But more interesting by far is the assessment of children who take up the challenge of making up their own games – they were challenged to:
- initiate their own activities
- use mathematical ideas to solve practical problems
- use appropriate mathematical language (cardinal, ordinal, comparative).

References and further resources

Alborough, J. (2002) *Where's My Teddy?* Walker Books.

Atkinson, S., Harrison, S. and McClure, L. (1997) *Seven Dizzy Dragons and Other Maths Rhymes (New Cambridge Maths).* Cambridge University Press.

Dunn, O. and Gon, A. (2003) *Number Rhymes to Say and Play.* Frances Lincoln.

Edwards, D., Garland, H. and Hughes, S. (2002) *My Naughty Little Sister.* Young Puffin.

Griffiths, R. and Millard, P. (1993) *Simple Maths Games.* A&C Black.

Grindley, S. and Thompson, C. (1990) *I Don't Want To!* Methuen Young Books.

Hutchins, P. (1997) *Titch.* Red Fox Picture Books.

Lester, H. and Musinger, L. (1995) *Me First.* Houghton Miflin Juvenile Books

Slier, D. (1998) *The Enormous Turnip.* Starbright Books.

Vipont, E. and Briggs, R. (1971) *The Elephant and the Bad Baby.* Puffin Picture Books.

theme: exploring the landscape

can you get to grandma's safely?

Here a familiar traditional tale acts as a starting-point for developing map-making skills and key environmental language.

And when you knock on the door I'm going to run away!

Grandma won't be able to run very fast.

You won't see me because I'm going to hide in the forest.

I didn't really want to be Grandma.

Before you start …

Key focus areas
The key focus areas are:
- Geography
- Language and communication
- Personal and social development
- Art
- Role-play
- Sharing ideas

Essential resources
The resources for retelling the story to the class were very simple, consisting of their own maps, which were blu-tacked to the wall so that the class could follow each group's story, and of course their puppets.
A range of materials was provided on one table for the children to make a large wall map. These included:
- Fabrics, wool, cards and papers
- Paints, crayons and pencils
- Scissors and glue.

Home-corner play
- Clothes for dressing up and acting out the story
- Playdough or similar
- Cooking utensils for making Grandma some cakes.

Small-world play
The children's own puppets can be used with their maps to act out the story. The children's maps could be laminated for outdoor use.

Other resources
Provide a range of maps for children to explore, together with photographs and pictures of landscape features.

Outdoor play
Children can have great fun using given props to act out the story in a wide open space. We used a large plastic play house as Grandma's house and made some signs to show directions, e.g. to Grandma's, to the wolf's lair, to the stream. We let the children use chalk on the playground and on an outdoor chalkboard to mark out and decorate their routes.

Planned outcomes
Children should be able to:
- take turns and share
- make and use simple maps
- develop relevant language
- sequence events
- offer ideas as to why Red Riding Hood got into danger.

Setting up the learning environment
- Fiction books that illustrate journeys; also other traditional tales, and non-fiction texts about trees and animals.
- A range of picture maps from stories
- Aerial pictures and maps of the school locality
- Puppet figures to cut out and colour, lolly sticks and sticky tape
- A table with a range of materials for cutting and sticking, and template shapes for features such as houses, trees, fence
- Large sheets of paper for group maps
- Colouring pencils and crayons.

Starting-points

'Little Red Riding Hood' is a well-known tale that is great fun to read and act out. It offers children the chance to engage with the story through role-play and to explore a range of landscape features.

Our starting-point
The children sat around and listened to the story of Little Red Riding Hood, taking turns to join in with role-play, and offering suggestions for the large map that we drew as we went along.

At the start of the story we discussed Red Riding Hood's house, and the children's suggestions were used to draw the house on a large board next to the storyteller's chair.

The children were told that we were going to make a map of Red Riding Hood's journey and that they would have to tell us what to draw and how to draw it. A child was chosen to come up and act out different parts of Red Riding Hood's journey. This section can include various landscape scenarios. For example, our Red Riding Hood had to climb a big hill, something our children are not very familiar with as we live in a very flat area. The child in the role did a very good job of huffing and puffing, and on advice stopped for a rest every now and then!

'And when Red Riding Hood reached the top of the hill, she looked all the way down to her house at the bottom and it looked so small.'

Comments and prompts such as 'What else can you see?' can help children to situate themselves in the 'landscape' and encourage use of words they might not be familiar with. By the end of the story we had completed our map and Red Riding Hood was exhausted.

Through the role-modelling of the mapping, we had given the children a clear idea of what was expected in drawing a map. In the next session they were given puppets to cut and colour, and paper for group maps. Introducing the concept of mapping is useful for two reasons: it provides a useful prop for children to use as an aid to retelling the tale, and develops a key geographical skill.

Productive questions
- What do you think Little Red Riding Hood's house is like?
- What do you think the path is like? Is it hard/stony/soft?
- What is a hill?
- What can you see from the top of the hill?
- How do you think Red Riding Hood felt when she went into the big forest?
- How do you think Red Riding Hood could cross the stream?
- Can you tell me about Red Riding Hood's journey/route?
- Where would you hide if you were the wolf?
- What do we need to put in our maps?
- What character would you like to be? Why?

Challenges and responses

Teacher-directed challenges
This setting provided opportunities for teacher-directed challenges focusing on:
- Imagining how Red Riding Hood would act on her journey.
- Development of landscape language, e.g. *tree, path, hedge, field, hill, stream*
- Development of positional language, e.g. *in, by, next, from, to, over*

Problem-solving
- How can we make a map to show Red Riding Hood's journey?
- How can we make landscape features for a large wall map?

Set challenges
The children were put into groups of three and given puppets of Grandma, the wolf and Red Riding Hood to cut, colour and stick. There were two key challenges:
- Can you decide by yourselves who is going to be Red Riding Hood, the wolf and Grandma?
- Can you make your puppets and work together to draw a map of Red Riding Hood's journey?

Child-initiated responses to the setting
In this setting, children were left with the raw materials to make maps and puppets. One group of three were arguing over who should

be Red Riding Hood. The teacher did not interfere but listened as she profiled aspects of the children's personal and social development.

Lucy: 'I want to be Red Riding Hood!'
Katie: 'No.' [clutching the puppet tightly]
Lucy: 'Please let me be Red Riding Hood!'
Katie: 'No.'
Lucy: 'You can be Red Riding Hood tomorrow.'
Katie: 'No.'
Lucy: 'I don't want to be Grandma.'
Alex: 'You can be the wolf if you want.'

In this exchange, Lucy tried every which way to get her wish while Katie would not even enter into debate. The boy in the group, Alex, was very quiet while this was going on, then offered his chosen puppet (the wolf) to settle the dispute. This exchange provided useful additional knowledge about these children's ability to share and take turns.

Further challenge
The children were given time to play with the puppets and their maps, which they enjoyed immensely. In addition, a table was set up with materials that they could cut and stick to make their own large wall map.

The next challenge was for them (in groups) to tell the story to the rest of the class, using the maps and puppets.
- Tell us who your characters are.
- What happened first? … next?
- Can you think of a different ending to your story?

Language

Key vocabulary
journey walk route travel path gate map view grass tree bush hill field stream river forest flowers valley wolf lair cottage house Grandma garden meadow wood woodcutter trunk start end direction arrive visit landscape scenery up to from at in next over through across under beneath scared quiet grassy flowing distance leafy walk skip run creep safe
bird names (choose one or two specific names, e.g. sparrow)

Encouraging children to use the language
Red Riding Hood went **through** the leafy forest, keeping to the **path**.

The wolf **crept** up to the tiny cottage.

From the top of the **hill** she could see across the **valley**.

Language across the curriculum
Personal and social
group share turn discuss safety rules obey danger rescue

Children's voices

Teacher: 'What are you drawing?'

Declan: 'Well … that's the flowers and the forest and … them flowers and um …' [points to features]

Jade: 'Grandma over there [points] and Little Red Riding Hood there.' [points to other side of map]

Declan: 'And all the trees and that's the path.'

Jade: 'That's little Red Riding Hood's house and that's Grandma's house and the flowers and the trees!'

Teacher: 'And have you made a puppet to use with your map yet?'

Frances: 'Yes we did!' [proudly holds up her puppet]

Teacher: 'Who is that?'

Frances: 'Well, that's Grandma.'

Teacher: 'Where is she going to be?'

Frances: 'Here, she has to go down here!'

[leans over and puts Grandma near a drawing of a house]

Jade: 'And that's going to be my house!' [leans across to the other side of the map with her Red Riding Hood puppet]

Frances: [ignoring comments by other child and continuing to talk about Grandma] 'She has to live down here in her house and she has to hide in the cupboard.'

Teacher: 'Can you show me where Little Red Riding Hood started her journey?'

Jade: 'In her house, here.' [points to her house on the map]

Teacher: 'So, what's this in this part of the map?' [indicates with her hand the path running between the two houses]

Jade: 'That's a zig-zaggy bit and I put all stones there and up there are some birds.'

Teacher: 'Oh, why did you make it like that?'

Jade: 'Cos it's a little bit of a hill!'

Declan: 'No, that's the path!'

Teacher reflections

'I had thought that I would draw something on the paper, possibly the path, as a reference point for the children's maps. Before I could do this, the children started drawing the maps very boldly. First they drew the houses, one on each side of the paper as I had suggested, then the path. I was surprised at the quality of the maps produced and the way some of the children worked collaboratively.

'While the children drew and played with their puppets and maps, I focused on a small group of children, listening to their comments and asking questions to see if they had grasped relevant vocabulary and were able to use a map to explain where things were.

'In this conversation, the children had were able to use key vocabulary and could identify features on the map. Frances was very confident in her feature language, map use and story recall. Jade used the phrase 'zig-zaggy', as I had used it in drawing the path on the map myself during the story, but appeared to be confusing it with the term 'hill'. Declan had drawn and identified features well, but showed less confidence in speaking, possibly because of the very confident nature of Jade.'

Further activities

Musical role-play
Collect sounds from made and found sources that can be used to accompany the journey through a forest, and encourage children to experiment with different sound effects. For example: leaves crunching, birds singing, wolf growling, footsteps and rain falling.

Small-world play
Using the map as a starting-point, make a three-dimensional model in found materials or papier maché.
- Can children make a bridge to get over the river?
- Can they make a place to hide?

Right and wrong
Discuss the issues in the story. Why did Red Riding Hood get into trouble? What did her parents tell her to do? Discuss and make safe rules for getting to Grandma's house.

Discuss how children help by running errands in their family, and what rules they have to keep them safe.

Family tree
Make a family tree for Red Riding Hood's family using children's drawings. Ask children to bring in photographs, or paint or draw pictures of their family and make their own family tree.

Sustainable development
Discuss how lucky Red Riding Hood was to live near a forest. Find out more about trees, and ask the children to choose a tree or trees to plant in their school grounds. Local organisations might be able to help with this. You could, for example, invite someone from a local gardening club to come and help the children plant a tree.

Look at trees in the area and try to identify them; notice their changes through the seasons. Explain that they are an

important part of our world and that they help to keep us alive and provide food and shelter for lots of animals. Have a paper recycling box in the classroom and ensure all paper waste goes into it. Appoint monitors to be responsible for this.

Your local council should have a recycling officer who can advise you. Ask if they have any recycling promotions going – in the past we have had free puppet shows with a green theme, and a visit from a recycling robot.

Wolves in the wild
Children need to be reassured that there is no danger of running into a wolf on the way to their Grandmas. But what can the children find out about real wolves? What do they look like? Where do they live? How do they live? Make a large collage of a wolf and find words to describe it. Use the internet to look at images of places where wolves live.

Seasonal change
When investigating landscapes it is great fun to use images that reflect seasonal change

and provide appropriate clothing for children's imaginary play and exploring. For example, this story can be set equally well within a wood full of bluebells in spring or a wood thick with snow in winter.

Eco-school
Join the Eco-school scheme and involve children through a school council. Contact your LEA to find out whether they have any schemes running.

Moving about
Use indoor or outdoor space to explore a range of movements that might be used on a journey: walking, skipping, wading, climbing, running, etc. Use *We're Going on a Bear Hunt* (Rosen and Oxenbury, 2003) as a template to make up a story to accompany the movements.

Circle time
Ask the children to say what makes them feel scared, and discuss solutions.

Assessment for learning

Geographical experiences can be found throughout the Foundation Curriculum, not just within Knowledge and understanding of the world. Good geography builds on children's natural curiosity and develops enquiry skills through first-hand experience and sensory interaction, clear and varied communication, critical questioning, and the ability to empathise with others. For example, children should be developing the ability to:

- ask relevant questions and suggest how they can find answers
- make connections, such as cause and effect
- share and communicate ideas in a variety of ways
- use photographs and maps
- think about others and the world around them sensitively.

Opportunities for assessing the attitudes, values, knowledge and skills relevant to geography exist throughout the six areas of learning. In the examples, drawn from the Foundation Profile, assessments are based on Communication language and literacy, Knowledge and understanding of the world, and Personal social and emotional development.

References and further resources

Bateman, D. (1996) *The Oxford Children's A-Z of Geography*. Oxford University Press.

Baxter, N. and Lewis, J. (1999) *The Three Little Pigs and the Big Bad Wolf*. Ladybird Books.

Eco-Schools website (www.eco-schools.org.uk)

Grimm, J., Grimm, W., Baxter, N. and Stevenson, P. (1993) *Little Red Riding Hood*. Ladybird Books.

Hutchins, P. (1970) *Rosie's Walk*. Picture Puffins.

Roffey, M. (1995) *How Do We Get There*? Macmillan Children's Books.

Rosen, M. and Oxenbury, H. (2003) *We're Going on a Bear Hunt*. Walker Books.

Sendak, M. (2000) *Where the Wild Things Are*. Picture Lions.

Images and sounds of wolves can be found on the following websites: Searching Wolf www.searchingwolf.com/videos.htm and look especially at the page with audio clips of wolf howls www.searching wolf.com/howls.htm which are great fun (download them into Windows Media and children can use earphones to click and listen) and Wolves wolves wolves (www.wolveswolveswolves.org).

Aims
- Recall a story in increasing detail, for example by sequencing cards.
- Use language to imagine, act out or develop experiences.
- Make and use a simple map.
- Identify some features and talk about those s/he likes and dislikes.

Teacher comments
Lucy, Katie and Alex were retelling the story of Little Red Riding Hood to the class using maps and puppets they had made. Lucy took the lead in the story and was sequencing it accurately using the features as landmarks. She then said 'And then the wolf jumped out from behind the trees' – at which Katie interrupted her with 'You forgot to pick the flowers!'

Alex could tell me what happened next when prompted but was too shy to speak in front of the class. I made a note to plan for opportunities and settings that would give him more confidence in speaking.

Several children found the concept of 'hill' difficult, so I planned the next day's activities to include modelling material to make a visual hill.

Aims
- Investigate places, objects, materials and living things by using all the senses as appropriate.

Teaching assistant comments
Ben wanted some material to make the 'water look shiny'. He explored the wool and then several pieces of material before choosing to use metallic paper. He asked me if it made the stream look like it 'was full of water drops'. Ben also worked very carefully in constructing his tree for the wall display.

Aims
- Look closely at similarities, difference and change.
- Begin to think about acting sustainably.

Parent comments
Harry told me that he has to check the paper recycling box and the bin every day in case it's got muddled up. He says that if we use too much paper then more trees will have to be cut down, and that's not good!

Teacher comments
Jade came running in the other day and said that she had seen flowers on one of the trees. She asked me if all the trees were going to get flowers on because the one she had made didn't have them.

theme: the living world

why won't my seed grow?

In this theme, the environment is used as a starting-point, as this helps children to develop knowledge, understanding and respect for the world around them. The direction taken in the activities resulted from the spontaneous interest shown by the children in their outdoor play.

Before you start ...

Key focus areas
The key focus areas are:
- Language and literacy
- Mathematics
- Science – living things
- Personal, social and emotional development

Essential resources
- A varied collection of seeds (depending on the time of year, you should be able to find acorn, conker, apple, avocado, coconut, cress, sunflower, sycamore, hazel, beech, runner bean, dandelion)
- Sorting hoops (or PE hoops)
- *The Tiny Seed* (Carle, 1997)
- Magnifiers of different sorts, especially large magnifying glasses and flexible magnifiers; an Intel computer microscope can also be used
- Small plant pots, lolly-stick labels, seeds and seed packets, compost, trowel, watering can and other garden tools, and till and price tickets
- Bean seeds and plastic cups
- Seed diaries – these can be cut out in the shape of a bean seed

Planned outcomes
Children should be able to:
- use simple criteria to sort the seed collection
- use their developing observational skills to find seeds in the outdoor play area and to begin to see fine details of seeds
- show understanding of the life-cycle of plants
- begin to develop respect for living things and learn to care for the growing seeds
- communicate ideas to others
- develop new vocabulary connected to growing seeds.

Setting up the learning environment
- Provide story and information books about seeds, including Eric Carle's *The Tiny Seed* (1997).
- Set up the role-play area as a 'Garden centre' for gardening and shopping, with space for counting out seeds for sale.
- Provide a table where the children can grow their seeds.

In addition, the provision of interesting resources in outside play areas can stimulate and develop children's learning, especially those with limited opportunities for outdoor play in their home environment.

There are big and little seeds.

There are seeds in apples.

Seeds grow into plants.

Starting-points

All environments provide opportunities for rich exploration: even urban areas with little or no grass and trees will have plants growing in pots and cracks in paving-stones. This theme was initiated by a child's interest in seeds and flowers which the adults then developed into learning about:

- sorting and classifying seeds
- using magnifying equipment to explore and observe closely
- using descriptive language and thinking skills to make predictions
- developing social skills and positive attitudes in growing and caring for seeds and plants
- counting and pricing items in role play.

Our starting-point

During outdoor play, the children began to pick flower and seed heads and use them in their role play, as money and food for a picnic. I noticed that Leanne in particular was looking closely at the seed heads, and gave her a flexible magnifier so that she could look at the finer detail. She went around the play area looking closely at small objects, including plants, flowers and seed heads. I suggested to other children that they might collect the flowers and seed heads so we could all look closely at them. We used the magnifiers to enhance their observations.

Later, I added other seeds to the original collection on a table with some sorting hoops. I asked individual children to choose one seed and to describe it in their own words, introducing and reinforcing the use of relevant vocabulary, such as *seed, round, grow, plant*. I then asked the children to find all the small seeds and put them into a sorting hoop on the table. All the big seeds went into another sorting hoop. Peter held up the coconut and said 'This is not a big seed, it is **very** big.' He was not sure where to put it, but Sara said 'Let's make a "very big" pile',

and with Peter's agreement we put the coconut into another sorting hoop.

During story-time, we read Eric Carle's *The Tiny Seed* and discussed the children's ideas about seeds and growth. Edward said 'You get coconuts at the Fair.' This prompted a diversionary discussion about the Fair. I asked Edward if he knew where the people at the Fair had got the coconut. He shrugged, but Rosie shouted out 'They're at the shops!' After some encouragement, she told us that she had seen some coconuts at the supermarket when she had been shopping with her mother. We talked about this, and other children were unsure whether they had seen any other seeds at the supermarket, so we all agreed to look next time we went shopping.

Productive questions

- How are the seeds different from each other?
- Are any of the seeds the same as each other?
- How can we sort the seeds?
- Can we sort them any other way?
- Do you think all the seeds will grow into plants?
- Do you think the big seeds grow into big plants?
- Where do you think the seeds come from?
- How should we look after the seeds to make them grow?

The big seeds will grow into big plants.

These seeds will all grow.

Big plants sometimes grow from little seeds.

All the seeds will grow if we look after them.

The roots will grow first and the shoot will grow second.

Challenges and responses

Teacher-directed challenges

This setting provided opportunities for:
- sorting and classifying seeds using different criteria
- investigating planting and growing seeds
- developing descriptive language and predictions
- working together to care for the plants.

The next day, I showed the children some seeds I had bought from the shops. They included herbs (basil, lavender, rocket), flowers (sunflower, poppy), beans and cress. We looked at the packets and the seeds inside, and talked about what would happen if we sowed the seeds. I added other seeds to the collection (acorn, conker) and some fruit (lemon, avocado and apple), and we looked at these and discussed if they would grow too. I reminded the children that not all seeds are safe for us to eat.

Set challenges

For the 'Garden centre' we encouraged the children to:
- collect seeds from home and bring them in to add to the collection
- choose some seeds of their own to grow
- grow bean seeds in plastic cups with blotting paper, and observe them growing
- write their names on 'lolly-stick' labels to

identify their seeds/plants
- remember to water their seeds/plants every day
- [some children] keep a diary illustrated with pictures of their seed(s) growing.

They were also challenged to consider:
- which seeds would grow into big plants and which into small plants
- what their seeds needed in order to grow
- what would happen if they did not take care of their growing seeds.

Child-initiated responses to the setting

During the sorting activity, several children sorted the collection of seeds according to observable criteria (texture, pattern, shape) and used good descriptive language when talking about the seeds. One child, Sara, used more sophisticated sorting criteria by suggesting a 'very big' pile in addition to the 'small' and 'big' seed piles. Many children used magnifying equipment (hand lenses and the Intel microscope) safely and effectively for close observation.

After they had planted their seeds, many of the children showed a positive attitude towards living things by caring for their growing plants. Some children showed prior knowledge of the conditions needed for plants to grow well (water and sunlight), although they were not aware that seeds need different conditions to germinate. Some children made decisions about which seeds to grow.

Language

Key vocabulary

seed grow plant root shoot water dry wet leaf soil petal flower pot seed heads (names of fruits and other seeds used, e.g. beans, acorns) big small tiny sunlight shade winter spring summer autumn

Encouraging children to use the language

We have to **water** them

They like the **sunshine**

Look at the **tiny shoots**

Language across the curriculum

Mathematics - comparative language of order and size

first second tiny smaller bigger very big

History - sense of past and present events

will grow have grown

Children's voices

Leanne: 'Look at these!' [seed heads]

Suzanne: 'This one's ten pence.'

Sara: 'I haven't got ten pence.'

Suzanne: 'OK. Five pence then.'

Afsan: 'That one's mine - I know 'cos I planted it and it's going to be a sunflower.'

Suzanne: 'You can buy it if you like. It's five pence - but you can't take it home yet 'cos it's my turn to water the seeds today.'

Afsan: 'All right - I'll just take it for a bit.'

Zoe: 'If we look after them they will grow big and strong.'

Dale: 'We got to water them!'

Suzanne: 'My Nana says they like the sunshine. She puts her tomato seeds on the window-sill.'

Teacher reflections

'Leanne instigated the work on seeds. During outdoor play-time she began to look carefully at the seed heads as she collected them. We provided magnifying glasses and encouraged the children to use them to look at the seeds. Leanne noticed small details in the seed heads and began to compare different seeds.

'In playing with the till in the 'Garden centre', the children showed an awareness of the value of the different coins. Afsan also identified her seeds by name, and Suzanne showed a sense of responsibility in turn taking and caring for living things.

'As they labelled the pots containing their seeds Zoe, Dale and Suzanne showed knowledge and understanding of what would happen to the seeds when planted and of the care needed to enable the seeds to grow. Suzanne drew on knowledge gained through her family's caring for plants in deciding where to place her seeds to encourage them to grow.'

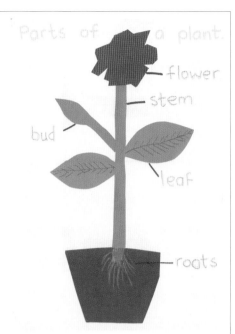

Further activities

Create a seed and plant corner as a hands-on display that the children can revisit at will.

Flower pictures

Work with the children to make pictures of a flower using different types of seeds or seed heads.

Place a flowering plant in the centre of the table and ask the children to draw, paint or produce collages of them. Talk about the parts of the plants and label them on the children's pictures.

Counting seeds

Count the seeds in the sorted piles – which is the biggest number? Which the smallest? Squeeze different types of citrus fruits (and extract seeds from other types of fruits) to extract the pips and count them. Why might some fruits have more seeds than others?

Rooting cuttings

Science: Take cuttings from a spider plant, put them in water and allow the roots to grow. Talk about the colour and shape of the roots.

Instruction manual

Language and literacy: Use a writing frame or drawing sequences to create instructions on how to plant and grow seeds. Encourage the children to look at their bean diaries when doing this activity.

Sound makers

Provide a variety of containers and demonstrate how the children can use different seeds to make sound-makers for music and rhythm. Which seeds make the best sounds? How does the sound change if you use fewer bigger seeds or more smaller ones?

The Tiny Seed

Use movement and musical instruments to dramatise the story of *The Tiny Seed* (Carle, 1997) – put on a performance for parents.

Assessment for learning

It can be useful to assess aspects of children's learning under the separate headings of knowledge and understanding (including the ability to apply knowledge in a new context), skills and attitudes. Children in this project showed a knowledge and understanding of: 'features of living things' and 'descriptive vocabulary'. In relation to skills they demonstrated an ability to:

- observe similarities, differences and patterns in the seeds
- explore, using all the senses in their observations
- sort according to observable criteria
- communicate and interact with others.

Their attitudes included: 'learning to care and show concern for living things' and developing 'self-confidence in exploring the meanings and sounds of new words'.

References and further resources

Boyle, A. and Rivers, R. (1999) *Jack and the Beanstalk*. Ladybird Books.

Carle, E. (1997) *The Tiny Seed*. Picture Puffins

Carle, E. (2002) *The Very Hungry Caterpillar*. Picture Puffins.

Cave, K. and Wulfsohn, G. (2003) *One Child, One Seed*. Frances Lincoln.

Hall, D. and Butler, J. (1995) *Baby Animals* (five stories of endangered species). Walker Books.

Hughes, S. (1998) *Out and About* (poems). Walker Books.

Hughes, S. (1997) *Rhymes for Annie Rose*. Red Fox Picture Books.

Hutchins, P. (1997) *Titch*. Red Fox Picture books.

Intel Microscope (2001) IntelPlay QX3. ANDNes/Science Corporation.

Matusiak, C. (1996) *Bright Ideas for Early Years: Seasonal activities: spring & summer/autumn & winter*. Scholastic Publications.

Woolfitt, G. (1995) *Science Through the Seasons series: Spring, Summer, Autumn, Winter*. Wayland Publishers.

Aims

- Talk activities through
- Identify features of living things.

Teacher comments

Leanne showed knowledge of living things in the environment by collecting seed heads and explaining to the adult what she had collected and where they had come from. She examined the seed heads closely and observed small details.

Aims

- Sort objects and talk about sorting
- Look closely at similarities, differences, patterns and change.

Teacher comments

Peter sorted the seeds according to given criteria ('big' and 'small') and identified a new criterion ('very big') to sort by. He was able to observe similarities in the seed collection. As he was sorting the seeds, Peter talked about the seeds and used appropriate language.

Aims

- Identify features of living things
- Initiate communication with others
- Be aware of the needs of others.

Teacher comments

Suzanne showed understanding of the needs of growing seeds. She told the teacher about her grandmother putting growing tomato plants on sunny window-sills. She planted a runner-bean seed and some cress seeds, and put them on a sunny window-sill; each day when she arrived in school she checked that they had enough water.

theme: the made world – construction

let's build

This theme takes the children's experiences of looking at a building site, and uses them to support problem-solving and decision-learning in a variety of areas.

plastic pipes or guttering. Use these, or plastic construction kits, to set up the role play area as a 'Builder's merchants', include hard hats and safety goggles.
- Set up a 'Designer's office' nearby with large sheets of paper, pencils, small rulers and colouring pens for children to design what the builder can build.
- Set up a 'design and make' area where children can design and then construct their own buildings or vehicles using construction kits, found materials, boxes and different joining methods.
- Provide a 'tinkering table' where children can safely explore different ways of joining things with different materials such as nuts and bolts.
- Provide a table with building materials for the children to handle and explore.

Before you start ...

Key focus areas
The key focus areas are:
- Investigating materials (science)
- Creative role play
- Designing and making
- Language and literacy
- Health and safety: safe behaviour and use of tools and equipment
- Healthy sandwiches

Essential resources
- A range of construction kits which contain pieces that are different shapes, have different ways of joining together, fit together without any gaps, include bricks, have doors/windows, and will make frames that stand up firmly
- sticky tape, masking tape, card/stiff paper, plastic, felt-tip pens, scissors
- books about buildings and vehicles.

Planned outcomes
Children should be able to:
- develop an awareness of the purpose of structures in the built environment
- co-operate with others in the design and make activities
- use language to develop decision-making skills
- investigate and evaluate the properties of materials

Setting up the learning environment
- Create displays of photographs (labelled with key vocabulary) of buildings in the local area. This could be extended to include interesting buildings elsewhere, including overseas, particularly if children are regularly visiting particular countries.
- Visit, with appropriate arrangements for safety, a builder's merchant. Bring back samples of small bricks, sand, timber,

Starting-points

Building is an activity that can be undertaken by all the children. Outside many children will have seen the construction of roads, bridges and a variety of buildings for different purposes. Inside, they can use these experiences to create a range of products, using a variety of materials, and overcome different problems.

Engage the children in exploratory talk and building through:

- reading *The Mice Who Lived in a Shoe* (Peppe, 1984); this book follows through the process of building a 'house', including the needs of the mice, the design drawings, building and the finished house
- exploring different construction kits, including how the pieces join together
- looking at pictures of different buildings and the people who build them.

Our starting-point

If possible, identify a building site where you and the children can observe from a safe distance. Alternatively, visit a building to look at the materials used (i.e. glass windows, wooden doors, brick or stone walls). In our case, just outside our nursery play area the children could see a huge building site which had appeared over the summer holiday. There were numerous buildings on the site, all different shapes and to be used for different purposes, including offices and a hotel. The children started to watch the site, and discuss the different things that they could see. A few

of them even remembered that the site was not there before.

The children wanted to see more clearly what was happening, so we planned a walk to the perimeter fence and how this could be done safely. The children thought it best to walk in pairs, each holding on to a coloured rope.

At first we simply let the children look, and guided the discussion that followed their observations. We then asked questions and pointed out things they had not identified. Key areas were:

- safety
- how the buildings were starting to be put up (foundations) or had been started long ago
- different materials
- people who worked there
- the vehicles on the site
- who the buildings were for.

The children noticed the yellow hats and fluorescent jackets worn by the builders. We discussed the choice of colours and asked if others would be good. A few children thought that black would be a bad colour to see from a long way away.

The children saw and described different signs. We asked them to think about why the signs were there. A few children were able to say 'to tell them', 'to show us', ' to stop us'.

The children were amazed at how deep the trenches for the foundations were dug, but were unsure why. Some huge frameworks were already in place, but most children did not understand how these frames or shells became buildings.

They drew on their knowledge of 'Bob the Builder' and his vehicle, without always knowing its name … Dizzy, Lofty or Scoop? They were encouraged to look carefully at different vehicles to see what each one did, what the particular parts might be for (e.g. the

scoop at the front of the digger), and how they moved. We talked about which ones might go on the road, and why others would not.

Children could see the builders eating their lunch, and thought that builders would eat sandwiches at lunchtime, just like them. They also thought that builders would be allowed to have chocolate bars and cans of drink. This led to a discussion about healthy eating and tooth decay.

The children took photographs. Most were aware that these could then be printed and displayed back in the nursery.

Subsequent visits focused on different aspects such as shapes and patterns, and frameworks and joining things.

Productive questions

- Why do people need to wear special clothes on a building site?
- Why do the workers wear short coats and not long ones?
- Why do you think the builders need boots?
- Why are their hats brightly coloured?
- What might the builders have for their lunch? Why? Is that good for them?
- Can you guess what the warning signs are telling us?
- Why do they dig trenches (long holes) to put the walls in?
- What is the big framework for?
- What material is in the window? Why has it been chosen?
- When do you think they will put in the doors and windows?
- How does each machine work?
- Why doesn't the truck have a roof?
- What will happen when it rains?
- Are the vehicles used for anything else?
- Do you see these vehicles on the roads? Why is that?
- Who do you think will use the building?

Challenges and responses

Teacher-directed challenges

This setting provided opportunities for teacher-directed challenges focusing on:

- problem-solving: could they build a wall in the sand tray that would stand up?
- sharing ideas and experiences – for example, discussing what healthy sandwiches they could make and making some of these sandwiches
- the development of technical language about the building site, the vehicles, and the tools and equipment they could see
- the development of understanding that products are for particular tasks or jobs, that people like different foods, and that safety is important.
- The children could create pictures and posters on these themes, to be displayed. For example, 'Always wear a hard hat on the building site!'

Set challenges

Having explored the theme through the initial visit to a building site, role-play in the 'builder's merchants', building walls, writing notices, and looking at books and models of vehicles, the children were given the opportunity to design and make a building using the construction kits. They were encouraged to think about:

- what their building would be for
- what shape it would be
- how they could make it stable
- what pieces they would use.

Child-initiated responses to the setting

Many children were able to recall and recount things that they had seen on the building site, choosing the experiences that excited them most.

All the children found something of interest to look at, talk about and follow up in different activities in the nursery.

Most of the children were able to identify different objects on the site, but few were able to articulate the different purposes and uses for the things they saw.

While the children could see and describe the trenches, many were unsure what they were for. However, when working in the sand tray with bricks, some of the children could see that by pushing the bricks down into the sand they were more firmly fixed.

The adults modelled answers to 'why?' questions, and this helped some children to think. Examples included: why the wheels on the vehicles were thick and wide, why the coats were brightly coloured, and why there were warning notices.

When they got back and started to look for things they had seen, some of the children found the books about buildings and vehicles.

Most of the children wanted to see the photographs they had taken, and helped to print them out. They were eager to look for the things they had found interesting.

In the role-play area they put on the hard hats and jackets and carried around pieces of piping, passing them to each other, as they had seen the builders do. This extended the children's vocabulary and gave them a real experience to talk.

Some of the children drew warning notices and put them up in the role-play area.

Further challenges

As the children explored the theme of building we gave them a further challenge back in the nursery: 'Design and make a coat for a builder':

- What colour would it be?
- What fabric would be suitable?
- What length would it be?

Language

Key vocabulary

brick piece join strong stable factory house office under pipe frame door window shape building slot wall roof overlap tubes   construction kit on top of   side by side

Encouraging children to use the language

The walls are **stable**; it is difficult to knock them over.
They build a **frame** first.
The bricks go **on top** of each other.
The pieces **slot together**.

Language across the curriculum

Mathematics

shape frame square rectangle long short tall size cylinder cuboid under side on top of

Science

push pull waterproof strong stable firm rigid

Children's voices

Teacher: 'What is your building like?'
Shanaz: 'Its walls are tall and wide. There is the door.'
Teacher: 'Who is it for?'
Shanaz: 'It's for me. I can play in it. It's got lots of colours. If I push it may fall down.'
Teacher: 'How did you build it?'
Shanaz: 'There is nothing on the top. I need more [bricks] to make it bigger.'

Teacher: 'What is your building like?'
Malachi: 'I am building my walls strong. They go in sand. My house won't fall over. I want a door. How can I put it on?'
Teacher: 'Who is it for?'
Malachi: 'It is for the builder [a toy figure]. He can go in when it's wet. Boss there.'
Teacher: 'How did you build it? '
Malachi: 'The holes are the windows. I have stuck my roof on. Blow away.'

Teacher: 'What is your building like?'
Polly: 'I got this one [construction kit] as it has tubes.'
Teacher: 'Who is it for?'
Polly: 'Mine is a big office.'
Teacher: 'How did you build it? '
Polly: 'Frame like the one there [points to the building site]. I got card and put it on for walls. Door stuck on. Look, door moves. Cold will go in the windows.'

Teacher reflections

'All the children wanted to use the construction kits together with some construction materials, even those who do not usually build with the kits. Most chose to build a house for themselves (like Shanaz) or for a toy figure; others chose to build an office, a shop or a shelter for the builder.

'They were encouraged to talk about their ideas first to clarify what they were going to build and who it was for. Paper was available if they wanted to draw any ideas. The time taken varied, according to their enthusiasm for the task and how easy they found it to build what they had envisaged. Adults intervened only when asked, and usually started by asking some questions. Some children were hindered by not having enough pieces to build what they wanted.

'The children had to make decisions about the type of building to be constructed, what materials they would use, how they would fit the pieces together, and how they would make roofs, doors and windows.

'While both boys and girls were excited by the walk and showed interest in the site, it was noticeable that generally it was the boys that chose to play in the builder's merchants and with the tools and dressing-up clothes. However, with encouragement the girls joined in.

'This experience provoked questions from almost all the children, without prompting.'

Further activities

Different buildings

Provide a range of construction kits and bricks that offer opportunities to build different buildings.

Ensure that there are opportunities to engage the interest of both boys and girls.

Our building-site book

Create a book using the children's drawings and paintings, and the digital photographs that the children have taken, to show how the building site has developed.

The builders

Ask someone from the building site to visit and talk to the children, showing them their work clothes. Encourage the children to ask questions, some of which could arise out of their visit to look at the site.

Stories and gender issues

Read both non-fiction and fiction books that include references to building and builders, especially *Sam and the Big Machines* (Henderson, 1987) and *The Mice who Lived in a Shoe* (Peppe, 1984). The Bob the Builder books and videos are also well known to many children. Ensure that there are both male and female role-models, e.g. Zahar Hadid who designed the Welsh Opera House, the Cincinatti Arts Centre. Focus on the structures and mechanisms and talk about what they are and how they might work.

Displays

Cut out silhouettes of tools and vehicles that the children have seen and that the builder might use.

Create a display of large-scale photographs of local buildings that have interesting shapes and are used for different purposes. Include photographs that show frames and shapes, for example, on the outside of buildings, bridges, playground equipment, cranes.

Put the children's model buildings on a display, together with their design drawings, pictures of whom the buildings are for and what they would be used for.

Show the children how to take rubbings of different building materials, either in situ, or of those that have been brought in from the builder's merchants and add these to the display.

Outdoor area

The children can make safety and information signs, which are then laminated and displayed in the outdoor area. Encourage the children to assess their usefulness.

Building materials

Children could explore different building materials such as drainpipes, sand, bricks and wood to find out about the properties of different materials, e.g. hard, soft, waterproof, rough, see through.

Children could test the strength of a wall by finding out which pattern of bricks is strongest.

Assessment for learning

These activities will provide opportunities to enhance the children's knowledge and understanding of the made world, to question, and to construct in a purposeful way.

The teacher needs to access the children's thinking through observation asking a variety of questions that could help them to make sense of what they have seen and to understand the reasons for the decisions that have been made.

Opportunities should be taken to assess other areas (where appropriate) of early years development such as language, mathematics and personal, social and emotional education.

References and further resources

Baxter, N. and Lewis, J. (1999) *The Three Little Pigs and the Big Bad Wolf.* Ladybird Books.

Bob the Builder series (various years, various authors) BBC Consumer Publishing .

Bonner, A. and Paisley, J. (1993) 'Mud' and 'The mud-pie makers rhyme' in Foster, J. (ed) *Twinkle, Twinkle, Chocolate Bar: Rhymes for the very young.* Oxford University Press.

Burningham, J. (1990) *A Good Job.* Walker Books.

Carle, E. (2000) *Papa, Please Get the Moon for Me.* Picture Puffins.

Cross, V. and Sharratt, N. (2001) *Sing a Song of Sixpence: Popular nursery rhymes.* Oxford University Press.

Henderson, K. (1987) *Sam and the Big Machines.* Picture Puffins.

Hughes, S. (1997) 'Castles' in *Rhymes for Annie Rose.* Red Fox Picture Books.

Hughes, S. (1998) 'Sand' in *Out and About* (poems). Walker Books.

Peppe, R. (1984) *The Mice Who Lived in a Shoe.* Picture Puffins.

Webb, A. and Fairclough, C. (1986) *Talkabout Sand.* Watts.

Yeoman, J. and Blake, Q. (1996) *The Do-it-yourself House that Jack Built.* Picture Puffins.

Aims
- Talk about what is seen and what is happening
- Identify the uses of everyday technology, through the use of the digital camera.

Teacher comments

Jemima was excited by the visit to look at the site. Usually quiet, she asked questions about what she could see, what the builders were doing and what the vehicles were for. Back in the nursery and for days to come, she continued to talk about the visit and ask other questions. Jemima also wanted to use the camera to record what she could see, and used the photographs, when printed, to remind herself of what she had seen.

Aims
- Ask questions about how things work
- Look closely at similarities and differences.

Teacher comments

Jed was able to talk about the different tools in the 'builder's merchants' set up in the nursery. He asked questions about what the different tools did and how to use them, before showing how he could use them. He was able to point to differences, and also to talk about them being the same colour and made of the same material.

Aims
- Build and construct with a range of objects
- Select an appropriate technique for joining.

Teacher comments

Sabina constructed a shop that sold sweets 'like the one on the way home'. She was able to select bricks that fitted together, and tried to overlap the bricks to 'make the walls stand up'. She chose a piece of stiff paper for the door so 'it was strong', and used tape to attach the door 'so it would move … it won't fall out'.

guess who's coming to tea?

This theme starts with one of the most popular areas of an early years setting: the role-play area. It is established as a dining area containing all the requirements for pretend cooking and eating.

Before you start ...

Key focus areas

The key focus areas are:

- Communication, language and literacy
- Mathematics
- Geography
- Design and technology
- Information and communications technology
- Personal, social and emotional development

Essential resources

- *The Tiger who Came to Tea* (Kerr, 1991)
- Invitation writing frames constructed in conversation with children
- Brightly coloured plastic cups, plates, knives, forks and spoons
- Large arrow signs pointing in different directions
- Selection of foods from different cultures.

Planned outcomes

Children should be able to:

- create invitations through shared writing and emergent writing
- write their own name independently
- indicate the route to their classroom by putting arrow signs in the correct place and with the correct orientation
- set the table with the correct requirements for each person
- collaborate to prepare food for a tea party in a safe and hygienic way.

Setting up the learning environment

Preparations included:

- setting up the Home Corner as a play 'house'
- placing a wide range of invitations in the Writing area for the children to fill in
- creating a display of food and pictures of food that might be eaten. We included some unusual types of food, and foods that reflected our multicultural society
- creating a display of books to do with food and teatime, such as *The Giant Jam Sandwich* (Lord and Burroway, 1988) and *The Doorbell Rang* (Hutchins, 1986).
- developing small-world play within the Home Corner by - adding a table on which were placed plastic cups, plates, a tea pot, etc; and – putting out a box containing finger puppets and dolls.

Starting-points

The home corner is always a popular choice with children and often they will become readily involved in the 'house': setting the tables for a meal, preparing the meal and serving it to whoever happens to be passing. This play involves children in collaborative play, decision-making, counting and matching. By providing a Writing area, and setting up Displays and Small-world play, it is possible to extend the children's play and thinking in a variety of ways.

Our starting-point

We read the book *The Tiger who Came to Tea* (Kerr, 1991), a well-known children's classic. The reading was followed by two discussions in circle time. In the first discussion the children focused on the story, making statements such as 'The tiger ate all the food so there wasn't any more' and 'They had to go out to tea'. They also asked questions about the story, for example, 'What's in the tin of tiger food?' and 'Where did the tiger come from?'. The second discussion also started with the story, but quickly moved on to relating it to the children's experiences. The children had been to friends and relatives for tea, so they were able to relate the story to their own experiences.

These could happen in one session, but, if time and/or concentration do not allow this, as two separate sessions with a second reading. The book will stand several readings.

Productive questions

These were of two types, the first few questions were directly about the storybook, the latter were aimed at linking it to the children's own experiences.
- Did you enjoy that story?
- What did you like best?
- What didn't you like in that story?
- Do you want to ask anything about the story?
- Have you ever had a tiger to tea?
- Tell me about any visitors you've had to tea.
- What happens in your house when visitors come to tea?
- What do you have to do when visitors arrive?
- Have you ever been to someone else's house for tea?

Language

Key vocabulary

tea invitation invite guest visitor entertain prepare time o'clock plates cups knives forks spoons sandwiches biscuits cakes directions map right left turn straight on please thank you eat drink

Encouraging children to use the language

What would you **like to eat**?
Would you **like some more**?
Have you had **enough**?
I'm glad you could **come to tea**.
Please come again.

Language across the curriculum

Mathematics - number and capacity
Is your cup **full** or **empty**?
How many plates do we need?

Geography
... the **way** to our classroom
... signs and **directions**.

Challenges and responses

Teacher directed challenges

Each area we set up involved a different type of challenge. The invitations in the writing area were designed to encourage a sense of audience and purpose for the children's writing.

We concentrated on the display of food and pictures of food that might be eaten, looking at it with the children, encouraging exploratory talk, for example:
- What is this?
- What does it taste like?

The book display helps develop the children's book-handling skills – turning the pages, reading a page from top to bottom, distinguishing between print and pictures, developing the beginning of a sight vocabulary.

The puppets, finger puppets and dolls were intended to help the children practice the language of social interaction.

In setting the table we encouraged them to match one plate to one doll and make sure everybody had a biscuit.

Child-initiated responses to the setting

The children had been to friends and relatives for tea, so they were able to relate the story to their own experiences. When they had people for tea some children volunteered that they have to help by putting their toys away. In preparing for the tea, they explained that they had to 'go shopping and then make the food' and greet the guests, and, as one child said, 'make sure they have enough to eat, take their coats'.

Later, some of the children took the finger puppets and enacted greeting, inviting the visitor into the house and offering some food: e.g. 'What would you like?'. They also ended the party by saying, 'Goodbye'. Other children spent time setting the table for tea: matching up cups to saucers and passing around plates of imaginary food and pouring tea.

Further challenge

After several days of using these resources we felt that the focus was beginning to get lost and play was becoming repetitive. We decided to provide more of a focus and to allow them to practise their new skills and

understandings in a genuine context. So the challenge was given to the children: 'Let's invite someone to tea.'

After much discussion and many suggestions, it was decided to invite the headteacher and the office staff to tea in the classroom.

A group of children composed the invitations while an adult scribed for them. Their questions included:
- How do we show who the invitation is for?
- What does Mrs Wilkes need to know?
- How will she know who the invitation is from?'

Children's voices

Scenario 1

Charlie: 'There's no more in there. It's empty.'
Jemma: 'I'm going to have a croissant and a hot dog.'
Charlie: 'That's a funny thing to have. I like hot dogs.'
Andrew: 'I'll pour some tea.'
Charlie: 'It's empty.'
Jemma: 'Who wants some toast?'

Teacher reflection

'To me this is a lovely example of the children engaged in parallel play and just beginning to move out of this and take notice of each other. Charlie's prime concern was with the kettle: he was very insistent that it was empty.

'Jemma was more concerned with the food and was eager to create a shared meal – she tried several times to find something which everybody would like to eat. Adult intervention in role as a guest in their play would help their tentative collaboration.'

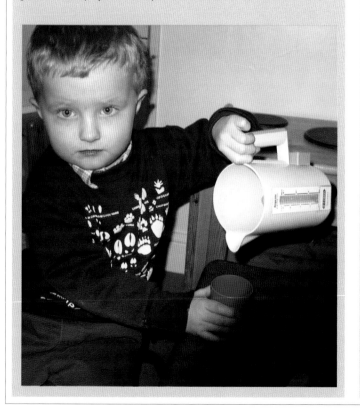

Scenario 2

Teacher: 'Where would you put this to show people the way to our classroom?'
Jack: 'Everybody knows where our classroom is.'
Teacher: 'But a visitor who came might not know.'
Jack: 'Then I would show them.' [pointing]
Teacher: 'But if you weren't there the sign would help them. Where would you put it?'

Teacher reflection

'Jack is perfectly capable of deciding where to put the sign, but he does not see the point of the exercise. He knows that everybody who comes into the classroom knows the way, and if they don't there is always someone to ask.

'This shows me how important it is to put each activity into a context which is meaningful for the children. This helps them understand the purpose of writing and the reasons behind symbolic representation.'

Further activities

Teddy bears' picnic

Set up or plan with the children to set up a teddy bears' picnic outdoors. The planning can range from where in the playground would be best to have it to what teddy bears might like to eat. Provide the necessary resources for them to set up the picnic for real (including bears, blankets, plastic plates and cups, etc.).

The science of making

Children could bake biscuits, cakes or make lollies for the teddy bear's picnic. Whatever they prepare focus children's attention on the changes in the ingredients (materials) and what causes the changes (mixing, heating, cooling). Take and print digital images for children to use to show the sequence of what they cooked or the changes that took place.

Constructing a barbeque

Work with the children to construct a small-scale barbeque using plastic bricks. The children can draw diagrams of this, labelling each part and then replicate the design in the outdoor play area, using larger bricks. The following questions can be used to stimulate discussion.

- Have you ever been to a barbeque?
- Tell me the sort of food you ate.
- Who cooked the food?
- Where did you have the barbeque?
- When do you think it's best to have a barbeque?

Lunch time

If food is prepared in the nursery setting, ask one of the cooks to talk about the weekly menu with the children. The children could look at the menu (if there is one) and make their own choices. What would you like? What do you think goes best with that? Have you ever had that before? What's your favourite?

My menu

Encourage the children to keep a record of what they eat over a day or two. They could colour in pictures, 'write' or ask an adult to scribe for them.

If a meal is provided in the nursery setting, the children could make a menu for a week to display. They could either do this on the computer using clip art and a word processing package or they could cut pictures from magazines and stick them onto a grid.

Going shopping

Arrange a trip to a local supermarket and look at the displays and conditions where different foods are displayed: the cold cabinet, dry goods, fruit and vegetables, frozen foods and fresh food counters.
See also 'It's my birthday' – pages 74-79.

Aims

- Listen with enjoyment and respond to stories.

Teacher comments

The children made their own personal response to the story. Amelia commented that she didn't know anyone who had ever had a tiger to tea. She was exploring the relationship between fact and fiction, and relating the story to her own understanding.

Assessment for learning

Much assessment of learning within the Early Years setting is based on informed observations of the children's behaviour. It is important to note the context of each observed behaviour, because some contexts are more conducive to more sophisticated behaviours than others. You need to observe the process as well as to analyse the final outcome. Attempts at symbolic representation can often appear meaningless without knowing what lies behind them.

Aims

- Write their own names.

Teacher comments

The children wrote their names at the bottom of the invitations. Joseph worked hard at forming each letter correctly and putting them in the correct order. He found it difficult to keep the letters small enough to fit on the marked line.

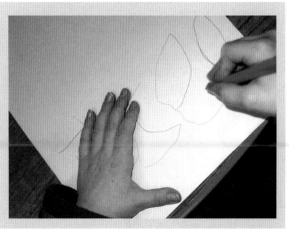

References and further resources

Burgess, L. (1995) *Bright Ideas for Early Years: Cookery activities*. Scholastic Publications

Carle, E. (2002) *The Very Hungry Caterpillar*. Picture Puffins.

Child, L. (2001) *I Will Not Ever, Never Eat a Tomato*. Orchard Books.

Hutchins, P. (1986) *The Doorbell Rang*. Greenwillow Books.

Hutchins, P. (2002) *Don't Forget the Bacon!* Red Fox Picture Books

Inkpen, M. (1995) *Lullabyhullaballoo!* (words and sounds). Hodder Children's Books.

Inkpen, M. (1999) *Kipper's Birthday*. Hodder Children's Books

Kerr, J. (1991) *The Tiger Who Came to Tea*. Collins Picture Lions.

Lord, J.V. and Burroway, J. (1988) *The Giant Jam Sandwich*. Piper Picture Books.

MacDonald, E. and Ayliffe, A. (1992) *Mr MacGregor's Breakfast Egg*. ABC/All Books for Children.

Milne, A.A. and Shepard, E.H. (1993) 'The King's breakfast' in *When We Were Very Young*. Methuen Young Books.

Vipont, E. and Briggs, R. (1995) *The Elephant and the Bad Baby*. Picture Puffins.

Aims

- Speak clearly and audibly with confidence and control, and show awareness of the listener – for example, by the use of conventions and greetings, 'please' and 'thank you'.

Teacher comments

The children used the finger puppets to explore how they might greet visitors to the pre-school. One said 'How are you?' and the other replied. 'Very well, thank you.'

Aims

- Look closely at similarities, differences, patterns and changes.

Teacher comments

The children chose cups and plates which matched in colour and commented on the pattern this made when they were put on the table. Lois drew my attention to the cups and bowls that did not match.

theme: counting and comparing

how many legs?

This theme takes a guessing game and uses it as the starting-point for a series of mathematical activities involving small-world activities, design and technology and information and communications technology.

Before you start …

Key focus areas
The key focus areas are:
- Maths (number, shape and space)
- Language
- Construction
- Information and communications technology
- Problem-solving
- Sharing ideas

Essential resources
- Models or pictures of animals/insects
- 'Magic box' to put the animals/insects in
- Playdough/modelling clay
- Drinking straws
- Scissors
- Modelling tools
- Junk materials, glue or sticky tape to make homes for the animals
- Animal books
- Internet sites for research on frogs.

Planned outcomes
Children should be able to:
- make a representational model with the correct number of legs
- talk about their animal and describe it
- begin to appreciate the elementary idea of symmetry and the pattern of even numbers.

Setting up the learning environment
- Set up a craft table where children can make a range of animals and include a small display of animal soft toys and books about animals. Show them how to make symmetrical monster pictures by folding painted paper in half.
- Provide books and rhymes that carry on the theme, such as *The Elves and the Shoemaker* (Grimm *et al.,* 1999), and 'There was an old woman who lived in a shoe'. In relation to this, we drew round both of each child's feet, cut out the shapes and wrote the child's name on them. (You can then either write large numbers on them to make a number line or leave them for the children to order (and using different colours for right and left accentuates the odd/even pattern).)
- Set up a table where children can act out the Noah's Ark story with toy animals, perhaps accompanied by an audio-taped version of the song – 'The animals went in two by two'.

Starting-points

Most children enjoy guessing games. This activity begins with a game in which the children guess the animal and subsequently make playdough animals with the right number of legs.

Our starting-point

We introduced the 'magic box', explaining that the children were to guess which model animals were inside it. (Using pictures rather than models may mean you can introduce a wider range of animals.)

For each animal we gave various clues – colour, habitat, diet, the noise they make, and special features such as horns or tails, as well as the number of legs. Experience shows that some clues are more useful than others. When the children had succeeded in guessing the animal, we took the model (or picture) out of the box to show them. We then put the models back in the box and encouraged the children to ask questions to which we gave the answers.

We wanted to focus on the number of legs each animal had. We chose two animals and asked the children how many legs each one had. Did they have the same number? Together we counted the legs and agreed as a group whether they were the same or different. We encouraged the children to describe the legs, prompting where necessary. We asked which was their favourite animal, and why, and indicated the picture books where they could look for others that we had

not yet mentioned. We then explained that they were to make a model of their favourite animal, using drinking straws for the legs. We deliberately restricted the modelling materials to focus the activity on the body and legs.

Productive questions

- What is your favourite animal? Why?
- Who has an animal at home? How many legs does it have? Let's clap that number.
- How many legs do *you* have?
- Do you think we can count all the legs in the room?
- Can you think of an animal that has short legs at the front and long legs at the back?
- How does … move?
- Why do you think the … has a fur coat?
- Why do you think the … has a shiny skin?
- Has anyone held a …? What does it feel like?
- What is the biggest animal you have seen? Where did you see it?
- What does … eat?
- Do you remember how many legs the spider had? Let's clap that number.

Challenges and responses

Teacher-directed challenges

This setting provided opportunities for teacher-directed challenges focusing on:

- counting and matching (the number of legs)
- comparative and descriptive language, e.g. *more, fewer, longer, shorter, smooth, furry, soft, shiny*
- positional language, e.g. *front, side, back.*

Set challenges

As the children became more and more engaged in their modelling, we suggested further challenges by offering additional problems and resources, such as:

- Are all the legs on your animal the same length? How do you know?
- Whose animal has the most legs?
- Is there an animal that doesn't have any legs? What is it called? Can you make a model of it?
- Where does your animal live? Can you make a home for your animal to fit in?

Child-initiated responses to the setting

- All the children were successful in using the limited materials available to make a model animal, although some were more identifiable than others!
- Some children used the tools to make their model animals resemble the real ones by giving an appropriate texture to the coat or skin.
- Several children realised that each leg matched another, i.e. that the animals were symmetrical.
- One child realised that some numbers were used each time while other numbers were never used, i.e. that animals always have an even number of legs.
- Some children drew pictures of their animal.

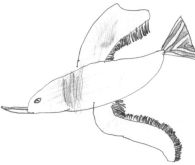

Further challenges

Once they had made their animals, the children were encouraged to talk with a partner about the similarities and differences between their two models. They then shared this with the rest of the class, and the teacher mediated the discussion in order to:

- encourage the children to use number words correctly, and
- encourage the use of comparative, descriptive and positional language.

Language
Key vocabulary

(number words) long short longer shorter feet toes legs body head water land air nest hole river pond pet wild furry smooth prickly scaly horns tail crawls hops slides jumps walks runs

Encouraging children to use the language
Mathematical language

short shorter long longer, more fewer

plus number words.

Talking about animals

Talking about animals could be extended by:

- showing a slide show of different sorts of animals
- watching a television nature programme
- drawing attention to classroom pets and discussing them
- reciting rhymes or songs that involve animals.

Language across the curriculum

English/literacy – descriptive language

Children's voices

Joe: 'Look at my horse – it's got … oh, it keeps falling over.'

Amy: 'Stick another straw in.'

Joe: 'OK. Oh no can't 'cos that's not the same.'

Amy: 'What?'

Joe: 'It has to be the same both sides, this leg goes with this one.'

Amy: 'Put another one in then, to make it stay standing up.'

Joe: 'Well, it can't be a horse then, 'cos the legs won't be right.'

Teacher reflections

'The children weren't working all together for this activity but in parallel. Listening to the comments and discussions taking place was very interesting, and provided much more information about the children's thinking than if we had just considered the finished result.

'Joe had the practical problem of having made a body that was too heavy and long to be supported by the straws. Amy's solution involved adding more scaffolding rather than redesigning the body to make it smaller. Joe's response showed he understood the need to match the legs, i.e. ensure that there were an even number, and that horses have four legs rather than any even number.

'Interestingly, Amy's initial model had an odd number of legs which were randomly attached to the body. After this discussion she removed some so that there were two rows of legs, although not the same number in each.'

Further activities

ICT activity

This activity provides opportunities for the children to further explore, informally, the ideas that the number of legs is even and that the two sides of the animal are matching. Use a paint program (e.g. *Kidpix*), set up with a mirror line to produce a symmetrical version of the child's drawing. Challenge the children to produce a picture of their animal or insect or monster, print it off and add it to a display with a label indicating the number of legs. When the display is complete, arrange a plenary session to discuss the pictures, drawing out the number of legs and the vocabulary for matching, e.g. same both sides.

Minibeast hunt

Carry out a minibeast hunt in the school grounds and count the legs of each minibeast found (snails - 0, ants - 6, worms - 0, spiders - 8, woodlice - 10).

Classifying animals

Look at classifying different animals according to their legs. For example, fish do not have legs. Snakes to not have legs, but birds have two legs. Lizards have four legs but their legs have scales on them, unlike dogs - they have four legs but their legs have fur.

Ask children to think about how different animals move using their legs, do they hop, run move sideways (e.g. crabs)? What are the feet like at the end of legs? Birds have claws, we have ten toes, horses have hooves, ducks have webbed feet for swimming.

Washing line

Provide an assortment of odd socks, and pairs of socks, of different colours, patterns and sizes, plus pegs and a washing line to peg them onto. Encourage the children to sort the socks into pairs; then add in an extra challenge: to line them up from smallest to largest, or to sort them according to colour or pattern.

The very long caterpillar

Make a zig-zag book with the children. Draw the face of a caterpillar on the front, and on each subsequent section draw a segment of the caterpillar. The children draw two legs on each of the segments and then have fun making the book shorter or longer, and counting the number of legs:

- Make the caterpillar longer. How many legs?
- Make the caterpillar shorter. How many legs?
- Can you make your caterpillar have four legs? Six legs? (Note: caterpillars have six 'real legs' like the parent butterfly, and also several pairs of 'sucker legs'.)

Fly like a butterfly …

Use the idea of moving like an animal as a focus for the physical education session. Initially, you could follow the format of a 'Simon says' activity (e.g. 'stand on your right foot', 'hop on one foot', 'jump with two feet together', 'stamp around the room') then develop it into a rich activity for extending the children's language. Make connections with the animals the children have made in their modelling activity. Offer them the opportunity to suggest the animals that the class could mimic, or let a small group of children perform a movement for the rest of the class to guess which animal they are portraying.

Whose shoes?

Set up a display table (or collect photographs) of different types of shoes. Use this as the basis for discussion about what shoes are worn by whom, when and where.

Whose feet?

Alternatively, set up an activity to match pictures of different types of feet with the corresponding animals, and discuss how feet are adapted for the habitat the animals live in.

Shoemaker

Teach the children the shoemaker rhyme (Atkinson *et al.*, 1997). Encourage the children to replace the animals in the rhyme with their own suggestions, and seek agreement from the rest of the class that they have identified the correct number of feet. The last verse provides a challenge for those children who are feeling confident with the idea of addition, but will not be suitable for all.

Shoemaker, shoemaker, make me some shoes,
I don't have any to wear.
How many feet do you have, little Ted?
Why two, can't you see them down there?
Shoemaker, shoemaker, make me some shoes,
I don't have any to wear.
How many feet do you have, little horse?
Why four, can't you see them down there?
Shoemaker, shoemaker, make me some shoes,
I don't have any to wear.
How many feet do you have, little ant?
Why six, can't you see them down there?
Shoemaker, shoemaker, make me some shoes,
I don't have any to wear.
How many feet do you have, spider dear?
Why eight, can't you see them down there?
Shoemaker, shoemaker, make me some shoes,
I don't have any to wear.
How many feet do you have, monster dear?
Why ten, can't you see them down there?
So the shoemaker worked all day and all night
To make shoes for his favourite friends.
How many shoes did he make, do you think?
Add two, four and six, eight and ten.

Assessment for learning

Closed mathematical questions may help you to understand what knowledge, skills and understanding the children have acquired, but are not in themselves helpful in furthering the children's learning. Combining challenging questions with observation of the children's responses can be more informative as well as more fun! In mathematics the teacher needs to access children's thinking by challenging them to:

- explain what they are doing
- use appropriate language
- look for patterns and relationships
- make connections between different parts of the curriculum
- find alternative methods, and solutions to problems.

References and further resources

Carle, E. (1994) *The Very Lonely Firefly*. Hamish Hamilton Children's Books.

Carle, E. (2000) *The Bad-Tempered Ladybird*. Picture Puffins.

Carle, E. (2002) *The Very Hungry Caterpillar*. Picture Puffins.

Cross, V. and Sharratt, N. (2001) *Sing a Song of Sixpence: Popular nursery rhymes*. Oxford University Press.

Crowther, R. (1995) *The Most Amazing Hide and Seek Numbers Book*. Wayland Publishers.

Dunn, O. and Gon, A. (2003) *Number Rhymes to Say and Play*. Frances Lincoln.

Grimm, J., Grimm, W., Read, L. and Hurt-Newton, T. (1999) *The Elves and the Shoemaker*. Ladybird Books.

Hughes, S. (1989) *Lucy and Tom's 1 2 3*. Picture Puffins.

Hutchins, P. (1970) *Rosie's Walk*. Picture Puffins.

Machin, S. and Vivas, J. (1990) *I Went Walking*. Bodley Head.

Morris, J. (1993) *The Animal Roundabout*. Dorling Kindersley.

Pienkowski, J. (2003) *The Animals Went In Two by Two*. Walker Books.

Pluckrose, H. and Fairclough, C. (1994) *Knowabout Numbers* and *Knowabout Counting*. Watts.

Yorke, J. (ed) (various) *My First Look at* (including: *Sorting, Shapes, Numbers, Seasons, Noises*). Dorling Kindersley.

Aims

- Extend vocabulary, exploring the meanings and sounds of new words.
- Use language to imagine and recreate roles and experiences.

Teacher comments

Luke took delight in the sounds of the words describing the actions he took when pretending to be a snake in PE. He noticed that lots of the appropriate words began with a 'sss' sound, and went on to invent others of his own.

Aims

- Find out about and identify some features of living things.
- Look closely at similarities, differences, pattern and change.

Auxiliary comments

Luke was fascinated by the life-cycle of the frog and wanted to replay the video clip over and over again. He gave an accurate running commentary, making comparisons between the stages as the tadpole changed into a frog, and using positional language correctly too.

Aims

- Use developing mathematical ideas and methods to solve practical problems
- Use language such as more and less to compare two numbers.

Parent comments

Christopher was very taken with the idea of two-ness, and spent much of the afternoon finding things that 'went together' or 'matched' such as shoes, gloves, cutlery. He sorted lots of other items into twos, and was very amused that an odd number could be too small to pair up, and too big at the same time!

theme: planning and making

the gingerbread people's day out

Children's experience of days out and holidays, real and imaginary, are used as a starting-point for a series of activities set in a multicultural social context.

Before you start ...

Key focus areas
The key focus areas are:
- Science – materials
- Language and literacy
- Geography – travelling and transport
- Personal, social and emotional development
- Problem solving
- Design and technology.

Essential resources
- An assortment of boxes in different sizes, cardboard tubes and other shapes, paper straws, assorted paper and pieces of card
- Scissors, single-hole punches, string, PVA glue and spreaders, a variety of adhesive tapes – clear, masking, parcel

- Laminated gingerbread people or the equivalent – dolls, teddy bears
- A copy of the letter from the gingerbread people
- Postcards, photographs, travel brochures, train, bus and plane tickets
- Construction kits, toy cars, buses, trains, aeroplanes, boats, etc., toy food
- Bubble mixture and hoops/straws
- Suitcases/travel bags and a range of holiday wear

Planned outcomes
Children should be able to:
- select materials for their designing and making
- join different materials together
- adapt the resources to suit the needs of their vehicle.

Setting up the learning environment
We used the range of resources outlined above to set up the following areas:
- toy vehicles (and track) on the

tinkering table for children to explore
- a 'design and make' area where the children can construct their own vehicles using found materials and boxes
- a food-play area for planning the gingerbread people's picnic
- displays, which included photographs of places to visit in the local area, cut-outs of buses, cars and feet to identify different ways of travelling around the local area; include questions and vocabulary linked to the stories and songs and books (e.g. *Mr Gumpy's Outing* (Burningham, 2001) and *The Big Red Bus Ride* (Curry, 1990))
- a 'Travel agency' with brochures and tickets for coaches, trains and planes.

The letter from the gingerbread people

Gingerbread People
Gingerbread Island
20th March 2003

The Nursery Children
Pinner Park Nursery
Pinner
HA5 5TL

Dearest Children
My name is Gingerbread Number 1.

Some of our Gingerbread people have asked me to write to you. We have heard that in your land you have days out to visit your favourite places.

We would like to visit one of your favourite places. Please could you send us the names of three places you think Gingerbread people would like to visit? Could you also tell us what we will need to take with us on our visit?

We will arrive in your nursery grounds soon. Could you please find us and make us feel welcome. We are small and flat and will need special transport to get back to Gingerbread Island. Can you help us?

Thank you.

With lots of love

Gingerbread number 1

We are going on a plane to holiday. Portugal.

We are playing on the sand.

Our room is big. It has three beds.

There are two swimming pools. One is little and one is deep.

Starting-points

Holidays or days out can give children a rich context for role play on journeys and travel. In circle time engage the children in talking about their holidays or days out, using, for example:

• postcards, photographs and drawings they have brought in
• suitcases and travel bags containing clothes, and items such as sunglasses, brochures and travel tickets
• displays and posters of different clothes for different climates and cultures.

Our starting-point

At the beginning of the autumn term we asked those children who had been on holiday to bring in postcards, photographs, etc., for us to talk about. We mounted the postcards around a world map, using string to locate where the children had travelled to. Where children brought in drawings and photographs we asked them to paint 'Our holiday' pictures.

Next, we passed round a bag containing items such as a flight ticket, a coach ticket, sunglasses, etc., as a starting-point for a role play about booking a holiday at a travel agency.

To extend the activity we used bubble-blowing to create 'magic bubbles' and gave

the children the start: 'My magic bubble will take me to …' Some children talked about going to the park or the shops as well as to India or Florida. We asked them draw their days out and added annotations as they talked about them.

During circle time we read out the letter from the gingerbread people. The children were familiar with the gingerbread people, which were laminated cut-outs, as they had used them before during a treasure-hunt activity. The letter told the children that the gingerbread people needed ideas for where they could go on a day out and what they should take with them. The children

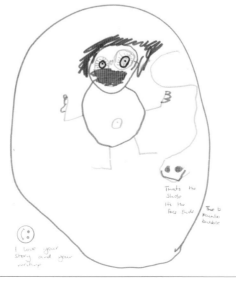

suggested some of the places we had already talked about, and each idea was written down on a piece of paper and placed in a bag. The three places chosen were: a visit to the park for a picnic, a model village, and the shopping centre. We also explained that as the gingerbread people were small and flat they needed special transport.

Productive questions

• What did you need to take with you when you went on holiday? Why was that?
• What do people need in a travel agency? Why do you think that?
• Where would you like the 'magic bubble' to take you? Anywhere else?
• Where can the gingerbread people go for a day out?
• How will they get there?
• Can you imagine and make a suitable transport for them?
• What will they need to take with them?
• How should they prepare for the changing weather?
• Where will they have their picnic?
• What should they take for their picnic?
• Who will be their guide or leader?
• Will they go one by one, or in pairs, or in whole groups?
• Will they need maps?
• Will they need mobile phones so they can keep in contact with the children.

Challenges and responses

Teacher-directed challenges

This setting provides opportunities for teacher-directed challenges focusing on:

- problem-solving: finding different ways to transport the gingerbread people and keep them safe on their journeys
- sharing experiences and ideas, choosing where to take the gingerbread people
- the development of language to describe holidays and days out, sequences of events, and weather conditions
- the development of understanding of forces and making things move.

Set challenges

Having explored the theme of holidays through role play, using construction kits and making story books, the children were given the opportunity to design and make their transport for the gingerbread people. They had to find out:

- how to keep the materials together
- ways to keep the gingerbread people safe on their travel
- any other ways the gingerbread people could travel to their island
- what the gingerbread people will feel when they get to their island
- ways in which they and the gingerbread people could keep in touch.

Child-initiated responses to the setting

In this setting many children were able to recall and recount with confidence the features of their recent holidays or days out, sharing their excitement with others. The children were also enthused by the idea of helping the gingerbread people, thinking of people in need.

This activity was accessible at all developmental levels, and individual children were able to follow their interests and use their creativity in designing and making their transport. Several children used construction skills with confidence, and co-operated with other in designing and making their transport.

The children valued each other's models. It was a pleasure for the teacher to listen to their comments, such as 'It's cool', 'I like your model' and 'That's good.' Talking through the process of making their models was the best outcome, particularly with children with English as an additional language.

Some children glued the gingerbread people to their model transport, which was not our intention but was logical if the gingerbread people were going to use these vehicles. Lisa incorporated seat belts in her design to stop the gingerbread people falling out of the vehicle.

Further challenge

As the children explored the theme of helping the gingerbread people to go on their day out, we gave them further challenges – for example, designing a picnic:

- What would the gingerbread people like to eat?
- Where would they buy the food?
- How would they carry it?

Language

Key vocabulary

box card big small join wheels round turn fly move stop wet dry join in on underneath side safe

Encouraging children to use the language

The gingerbread people need to keep **dry.**

We need to **join** these boxes.

The wheels are **round.**

The gingerbread people need to be kept **safe.**

Language across the curriculum

Science

wet dry waterproof rough smooth sticky shiny bumpy spiky hard soft

Mathematics

big small tiny square round rectangle sphere cuboid sides faces corner area quantity one two long short same size

Children's voices

Lisa: 'It's a car, but I haven't done any wheels yet. I will when I finish painting it. It's a boat too. It turns into a boat when it sees water. I putted some wheels. I made seatbelts, too, so they don't fall out.'

Roshni: 'It's nice, so nice. Can I take it home tomorrow?'

Lisa: 'I did this boat so they can get home. I found a box, put them [gingerbread people] on. Tahib put it [sail] on boat. They get in the boat, then they sail to their island. It's very cool.'

Roshni: 'I made a Barbie car for gingerbread man to go his island. I get box and do this [pointing to lids] make wheels. I do like this [matchsticks]. That door [lollypop stick]. That window [pasta].'

Teacher reflections

'The children understood the task and fully enjoyed this activity – they had a purpose and wanted to help the gingerbread people to get to their island. All the children spent no less than 35 minutes on the task. They were interested and enthused, and had fun making the gingerbread people's transport. The work required imagination and creativity – rich experiences. The children who created their transport first provided the motivation for the others.

'The children learned to use tools (e.g. scissors, single-hole punch) and become efficient with them. They also learned about how best to join things, and what resources would be best to use to make their transport.

'They were problem-solving all the time. For example, when the wheels of Roshni's transport slid off, both her and Lisa thought of strengthening the connection between the wheels and the box by using sticky tape. The art straws that Roshni used were very long, but needed to be slid through the box to make axels for the wheels. The children had to work out how to slide the straws through the long box. The straws needed to be measured and cut to appropriate lengths, and Roshni had to ask someone to help her hold the straw while she taped it.

'The children also had to talk through the process of making their models; they used phrases such as "I think" and "Maybe if". The children also developed evaluative designing and making language, for example, "This is not good glue. I'll use sellotape". When the children talked about their models they said:

- what they thought of their end-product, and
- what they thought of their peers' end-products while working in a group and as a whole class.'

Further activities

Different vehicles

Encourage the children to explore the space inside the boxes. Help them to open the boxes to see if the gingerbread people (or small dolls/figures) can fit inside for their journey.

Set up the water tray to allow the children to test materials to see which of them will keep the gingerbread people dry.

Provide construction kits which allow children to explore building different types of vehicles.

Wheels

Place a range of toy vehicles (such as cars, buses and aeroplanes) on the tinkering table, where children can investigate the movement of the wheels. If possible, put a short ramp nearby for testing how the wheeled toys will travel.

Send cars down the ramp onto different materials and see how far a car can go on carpet or across sand or a smooth surface like linoleum. Which surface is the best for cars to travel on? Find out which car goes the furthest. Is it a sports car, a family car or a truck?

Display

Set up a display of photographs of places to visit in the local area, e.g. the park, the high street and the garden centre – and use to create a pictorial map.

To identify different ways of travelling around the local area silhouettes of buses, coaches and cars can be mounted on the display board.

Children can paint pictures of the different vehicles to add to the display, alongside photographs of the models they made in the construction area and the outside play area.

Add a range of questions such as 'How many wheels does the bus have?', 'Where is the bus going?' and 'How can you get to the park from the High Street?'.

Outdoor play

Challenge the children to build a bigger vehicle, e.g. a fire engine, in the playground. Provide a range of materials, e.g. tyres, wooden boxes, plastic barrels and lengths of wood and tubing and dressing up clothes as appropriate.

Our holiday book

Make a book with drawings that the children have produced when they have been on a day trip or holiday. Include in it a 'passport' with details of their height, age, where they live and a picture of themselves.

Travel noises

Sing and do the actions for songs related to travel, e.g. 'The wheels on the bus'.

Work with the children to devise a journey of noise using voices and musical instruments. For example, in the country the children could make the noises of tractors and animals; in the town they could think about how to produce the noises of, e.g. buses, cars, lorries, pedestrian crossings. Decide on the order of your journey and then 'play' it through.

Choosing what to take

Put out empty suitcases together with a range of clothing, e.g. winter and summer clothing, protective headwear, tickets and sunglasses, and encourage the children to practise packing and unpacking the suitcases for holidays in different places.

Travel agents

Invite someone from a local travel agency in to talk about their job. Ask them to act out taking a booking using language appropriate for the children.

Aims

- Build and construct using a wide range of objects
- Show a developing understanding of ways to shape and assemble materials.

Teacher comments

Liza recognised that her vehicle needed to have wheels if it was to be a car. She put the wheels on after she finished painting it. She also wanted her car to change into a boat. To keep the gingerbread people inside the car she attached seatbelts made from paper straws. She was very pleased with her vehicle and wanted to take it home the next day.

Assessment for learning

We should look at assessment from the point of view of what it can do to enhance the experience of learning science (de Bóo, 2000). In science the teacher needs to access children's thinking by challenging them to:

- ask questions about why things happen and how things work, and
- look closely at similarities, differences, patterns and change.

References and further resources

Burningham, J. (2001) *Mr Gumpy's Outing.* Red Fox Picture Books.

de Bóo, M. (2000) *Action Rhymes and Games.* Scholastic.

Curry, P. (1990) *The Big Red Bus Ride.* Picture Lions.

Grant, G. and Hellard, S. (1994) *Little Blue Car.* Orchard Picture Books.

Oxenbury, H. (various) *Tom and Pippo series (including ... and the Washing Machine, ... Read a Story, ... Go Shopping, ... In the Snow, ... Go for a Walk).* Walker Books.

Rockwell, A. (various) *Cars, Trucks.* Picture Puffins.

Roffey, M. (1995) *How Do We Get There?* Macmillan Children's Books.

Rosen, M. and Oxenbury, H. (2003) *We're Going on a Bear Hunt.* Walker Books.

Southgate, V. (ed) (1982) *The Gingerbread Boy.* Ladybird Books.

Tanner, G. and Wood, T. (1995) *In the Street.* A&C Black.

Tanner, G. and Wood, T. (1995) *Eating.* London, A&C Black.

Aims

- Identify some features and talk about those features
- Select appropriately from resources offered.

Teacher comments

Ruaran was able to identify the key features of an aeroplane, relating this to one of the models he'd explored earlier. He was also able to select different materials to use and join them together using glue.

Aims

- Shows interest and enthusiasm and is motivated to learn.
- Uses language purposefully to explain
- Construct in a purposeful way, using simple tools and techniques.

Teacher comments

Danielle chose to design and make a boat to get the gingerbread people home. She found a box and glued the gingerbread people to the top of the box. Nikhil helped her put the sail on.

Parent comment

Danielle was really proud of her model when she brought it home to show us. She explained how she had used glue, straws and sticky tape to make the sail.

theme: investigating foods

it's my birthday!

This theme takes a children's birthday party and uses it as the starting point for a series of activities – culminating in exploring jelly.

Before you start ...

Key focus areas
The key focus areas are:
- Science
- Language
- Cookery
- Problem-solving
- Sharing ideas

Sensitivity, safety and care
When planning for any experience involving foods, it is important to show sensitivity towards the children's backgrounds, their allergies and religious or dietary needs. For example, some children are not permitted to eat jelly made with gelatine or ice cream made with milk products. Letters sent to parents in advance will give them the opportunity to advise you of any special needs and allow you to differentiate without discrimination. For example, providing a bowl of vegetarian jelly to explore alongside the other jelly tray, providing rubber gloves for *all* the children to use, making banana milk shakes with soya milk as well as cows milk. This will also encourage children to recognise and value each other's cultural differences.

The jelly is best used in a bowl. The longer jelly is handled the more unpredictable it becomes as a substance and it is less easy to control. Some jellies will turn the children's hands the colour of the jelly used, but this washes off.

Essential resources
- containers of different shapes and sizes
- different spoons for stirring and pouring
- jelly mix (crystals and/or cubes)
- jelly moulds
- plastic bottles, pouring jugs, sieves
- spoons with holes, vegetable masher
- large plastic boxes or bowls

You grow on your birthday.

No you don't, you grow at night.

I'm going to be five soon!

For my birthday we're going to have a bouncy castle.

Planned outcomes
Children should be able to:
- experience the physical characteristics of jelly as a material substance
- work collaboratively and talk about their experience
- experience using different pieces of equipment.

Setting up the learning environment
Create a science bag with items that children have for birthdays and parties as prompts for discussion – for example, birthday cards, birthday badges with age on, party bags, streamers, poppers, party hats, and storybooks such as *Kipper's Birthday* (Inkpen, 1999).

Create a 'Come to my party' area in the role-play area using, e.g. balloons, cards, presents, parcels, pretend party food and drinks.

Create a background display showing a party with lots of children, a birthday cake, balloons with ages on, and streamers.

Make a large 'pretend' birthday cake with mock icing, 'Happy Birthday' written on, candles, and place lots of questions around the cake, such as:
- What kind of cake do you like?
- How many candles should be on your birthday cake?

Explore, sing and play music and songs associated with different kinds of celebrations: birthdays, Diwali, Eid, Hannukah, Chinese New Year, Christmas, etc.

Make a large wall calendar and record the dates of the festivals.

Starting-points

The science story bag

A good start point is to show the children items from a science story bag and focus on the 'science' of each item. For example:

Party poppers

- What are they?
- What do they do?
- How do you think they work?
- What sound do they make?
- How do you think all the streamers are put into the popper?

Health and safety note: *Set off the poppers well away from children's faces.*

Party candles

- How many candles will be on your cake?
- What happens when a candle burns? – let's see.
- Why is it dangerous to touch a lighted candle?

Party blowers

- What sound do the party blowers make?
- How do you think they work?

Our starting-point

We have a particular month when a lot of children in the class have their birthdays. So we decided to change the 'Role play area' into a 'Come to our party area'. Inside this we placed lots of things that children have at a party.

We also placed lots of photograph albums that parents have helped us put together with pictures of their children. Many of the photographs show the children at their own birthday parties and at other family celebrations or festivals. Children enjoy looking at their own photographs as well as those of others.

We provided headphones and audio tapes of party music for children to listen to, and opportunities to play (with adult helpers) different games such as 'Simon says', focusing on the children learning, for example, words for parts of the body: e.g. *elbow, knees, wrist,* as well as more basic vocabulary such as *head, leg* and *arm.*

During the time that we explored this topic the children made different party foods such as party drinks, ice lollies, cakes, sweets and fruit salads, and savouries such as potato straws, pizzas, sandwiches and avocado dip with celery, pepper and carrot sticks. The children also made jelly.

While the children were cooking or preparing the food we focused on what our senses can tell us, so they used touch, taste, smell, sight and hearing ('look and listen') before and after cooking. We observed and described how things change, and what causes the change, and thought about how we could stop the changes.

Productive questions

- What kind of food do you have at your party and family parties?
- What is your favourite food?
- Why do you think we need to wash our hands before cooking?
- How did the popcorn change when we put the corn in the popper?
- How did we make the fruit salad?
- What did we do to make the chocolate strawberries?
- How do you think we could make different coloured jellies?

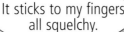

When I hold my fingers up it drips off.

Jelly is like snow 'cos its squashy.

It sticks to my fingers all squelchy.

When you drop it, it goes splat.

Challenges and responses

Jelly in the box (or 'jelly tray' as it became known) is such an excellent experience for young children. For once they have permission to 'play' with a food substance, one that has such a wonderful texture and does strange things when poured and touched.

Teacher-directed challenges

We filled the tray with cold jelly and nothing else to begin with. Just allow the children to feel the texture by running their fingers through it, squishing it in their hands, putting their arms in up to the elbows, and generally just experiencing the feel of this substance. This provided opportunities for teacher-directed challenges focusing on:

- Experiencing a different material using their sense of touch.
- Exploring jelly using a range of equipment and everyday objects.
- Working together by sharing ideas and helping each other – for example, one child holding a funnel and another pouring jelly through it.
- The development of exploratory language related to the task such as *wobble, cold, slippery.*

Set challenges

Either as the children were exploring or during a 'show and tell' session, we asked the children to describe how the jelly felt. We celebrated new words, even if they were not 'real words', that the children created to try to explain their experiences. We talked to the children about the properties of jelly – that it is soft, wobbly, nearly see-through, cold, not solid, not liquid like water, but it can be poured, it does fill containers, and it can be moulded.

As children worked with increasing confidence in the 'jelly tray', adults in the classroom intervened with further challenges by offering children different items to explore the jelly with:

- What happens if you try to put jelly through this sieve?
- How can you fill the lemonade bottle with jelly?
- What can you find that will sink in the jelly?

Child-initiated responses to the setting

In handling the jelly, some of the children liked the feel of the jelly, e.g. 'Blobby, I love it'; they also made observations about it's properties, e.g. 'soggy and wobbly', 'wibble wobble'. Others were not so keen – saying 'it's horrid – all gooey' and the same child observed how when squeezed it through her fingers, 'it squelches out'.

Once we provided them with a number of tools for investigating the properties of the jelly, the children began to explore further. They used a vegetable masher and a funnel in a number of ways. Ben observed that if he pressed the masher 'really hard, it goes through the holes'.

With the funnel first they simply squeezed the jelly through, but when prompted they began to use it to fill a lemonade bottle provided. Meanwhile, Jack placed his funnel upside down in the jelly and pressed it down. He then described how 'the jelly pumped through one of the holes like a volcano'.

Children's voices

Ashya: 'Nice.'

Terri: 'Smell fruity, strawberry.'

Ashya: 'Want to eat it.'

Elliot: 'Sticky.'

Ashya: 'Mint [meaning good], gooey, wobbly.'

Terri: 'I like jellies – I like the red ones best.'

Teacher reflections

'First of all we made jelly: each group made a different flavour, enough so that everyone could have a taste. It always surprises me how many children do not help to cook at home, so not only was there a science focus on changes but also basic hygiene and following instructions.

'With some groups I used jelly crystals, with others jelly cubes. We were able to compare what they both tasted like and decide which one was best. Tasting the jelly was fun for the children.

'The children were fascinated with the idea that we could make the jelly any shape we wanted, and I managed to get lots of different jelly moulds as well as using a range of containers of different shapes and sizes so that children could choose which shape they wanted. This brought in lots of mathematical language linked to shapes.

'Interestingly, the children did not have a lot of language to describe what happens before, during and after changes, so many new words were introduced such as *liquid*, *change*, *heat*, *wobble*, *flavour*, as well as *before* and *after*.

We used small jelly cases and plastic spoons so everything was disposable – another new word. It made me realise that children can learn quite complex words if given the opportunity.'

Language

Key vocabulary

jelly soft change liquid feel squish cold heat wobble pour feel slippery squelch slurp yucky runny flow slither bouncy smooth sieve jelly-babies spoon juicy wibbly flavour

Encouraging children to use the language

I can **pour** jelly

Jelly feels **slippery**

Jelly tastes **juicy**

Language across the curriculum
Mathematics

in through inside more less measure spoonfuls cupfuls

Further activities

Party music

Talk about party music, and play different kinds of music from pop songs to party-game music. Challenge children to make their own party music or sounds for a game – for example, a steady beat of a drum for 'pass the parcel': when the drum stops the person holding the parcel can take a layer of wrapping off.

Party video

There are a number of relatively cheap hand-held video recorders and instant or digital cameras that very young children can use safely and effectively. When you have a class party, or when cooking with the children, allow a child to video what's happening and another to provide a commentary – the video need only be a couple of minutes long – then show it to the class. Gradually children will become more expert in handling the video recorder or camera and will be confident enough to decide when they want to use it.

Banana milkshake

Let the children help you make a banana milkshake. Cut up the banana and allow them to measure out the milk and a spoonful of ice cream. You (not the children) should put the

ingredients into a blender and switch it on then ask the children to watch how the mixture changes. Allow them to drink some and discuss what it tastes like. Can they taste the milk, the banana and the ice cream? Could we get any of the ingredients back? The latter question is one that lays the foundation for understanding reversible and irreversible change.

Healthy party

With the children, talk about having healthy food at parties such as cheese, dips and vegetables rather than crisps, and milk shakes rather than fizzy drinks. Work together to design a healthy party menu and make some of the food.

Party games

Challenge children to make up their own party games that have a theme, such as blowing (using the force of moving air), e.g. blow football (use straws and a ping-pong ball), Flip the Kipper (flip a paper fish over on the table), and keeping a balloon up in the air without touching it.

The best ice pops

Show children ice pops, and ask them how they think they are made. Make ice pops or cubes of different flavours and different

shapes. Talk about what happens when they are made, using language such as *freeze, melt, cold, fridge, freezer, warm, liquid, solid, ice.*

Parents welcome

Invite parents to come in at festival times to help the children make or show traditional foods and costumes, e.g. make Easter bonnets and then have a parade.

Aims

- Investigate materials by using all of their senses as appropriate.
- Continue to be interested, excited and motivated to learn.

Teacher comments

Molly was keen to engage in exploring the jelly, and used many of the different utensils to find out what jelly would do. Molly showed curiosity when she asked to try other pieces of equipment from around the classroom and was eager to talk to other children and adults about the jelly in the bowl.

Assessment for learning

We should look at assessment from the point of view of what it can do to enhance the experience of learning science (de Bóo, 2000). In science, the teacher needs to access children's thinking by challenging them to:

- explain what they are doing,
- suggest the reason for doing something,
- make connections, such as cause and effect,
- share ideas.

Opportunities should be taken to assess other areas (where appropriate) of early years development such as language and personal, social and emotional development.

Aims

- Look closely at change
- Extend their vocabulary, exploring the meanings and sounds of new words.

Auxiliary comments

When we made the jelly, Ben was able to answer questions about how the jelly changed as we made it. He used new words, linking them to using his senses of sight, taste, smell and touch to find out about the jelly, and he made statements such as: 'The jelly in the packet is harder, like jelly babies', 'The hot water made it go all gooey' and 'Look – the water's going all red.'

References and further resources

Armitage, R. and Armitage, D. (1994) *The Lighthouse Keeper's Lunch*. Scholastic Hippo.

Bradman, T. and Riche, C. (1993) 'The sandwich' and 'The wobbling race' (jellies) in Foster, J. (ed) *Twinkle, Twinkle, Chocolate Bar: Rhymes for the very young*. Oxford University Press.

Burgess, L. (1995) *Bright Ideas for Early Years: Cookery Activities*. Scholastic Publications.

Foster, J. and Rosen, M. (1996) 'When Susie's eating custard' and 'I don't like custard' in Foster, J. and Thompson, C. (eds) *First Verses: Finger rhymes*. Oxford University Press.

Hughes, S. (1997) 'Teatime' in *Rhymes for Annie Rose*. Red Fox Picture Books.

Hutchins, P. (2002) *Don't Forget the Bacon!* Picture Puffins.

Inkpen, M. (1999) *Kipper's Birthday*. Picture Knight.

Kerr, J. (1991) *The Tiger Who Came to Tea*. Hodder Children's Books.

Randall, R. and Pochon, L. (1999) *The Little Red Hen*. Ladybird Books.

Royston, A. and Riddell, E. (1995) *Getting Better*. Frances Lincoln.

Stewart, K. and Shepard, E.H. (1991) *The Pooh Cook Book*. Mammoth Books.

Aims

- Use ICT to support learning
- Be confident to try new activities, initiate ideas and speak to a familiar group.

Teacher comments

We had used the digital video to take short clips of the children in the water tray exploring the jelly. Marcus decided that he wanted to video Sam pouring jelly out of a container and 'splattering' it, as he said, into the other jelly in the tray. He made his video and was really proud when he showed it to the rest of the class.

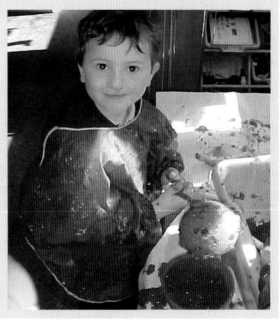

theme: the wider world

a basket of fruit from Kenya

This theme takes a popular children's story, Handa's Surprise, and uses it as the starting-point for developing attitudes, skills and knowledge about the wider world.

Before you start ...

Key focus areas
The key focus areas are:
- Geography
- Language and communication
- Personal and social development
- Art
- Problem solving
- Sharing ideas

Essential resources
The big picture book *Handa's Surprise* by Eileen Browne (1997).

Home corner play
- Basket or bucket and plastic fruit
- Dressing-up materials
- Travel bag and accessories

Small world play
- Table-top play map
- Model animals and sand tray

Other resources
- Blow-up globe
- Photo pack
- Map of the world
- World jigsaw

Outdoor play
- Small plastic buckets for collecting fruit peel.
- Simple map of the world showing continent shapes painted on playground including painted compass.

Planned outcomes
Children should be able to:
- think about their own and other's feelings
- begin to think globally and develop relevant vocabulary

- use their senses and first hand experience to think about likes and dislikes.
- explore and share their thoughts and ideas.

Setting up the learning environment
The learning environment can be varied to include opportunities for indoor and outdoor play, as described above.

Handa's Surprise
Handa's Surprise by Eileen Browne (1997) is a story that children love because of its predictable format and child-centred images.

Handa puts seven delicious fruits in a basket to take to her friend, Akeyo. But as she walks, carrying the basket on her head, various creatures steal her fruits. A monkey takes the banana, an ostrich the guava, a

Illustration from Handa's Surprise by Eileen Browne. © Eileen Browne. Reproduced by permission of Walker Books Ltd, London SE11 5HJ.

zebra the orange, an elephant the mango, a giraffe the pineapple, an antelope the avocado, and a parrot the passion fruit. Handa walks on, wondering which of the fruits Akeyo will like best, oblivious to the fact that her basket is now empty. But then, behind her, a goat charges into a tangerine tree and fills Handa's basket with the fruit. 'Hello, Akeyo,' she greets her friend. 'I've brought you a surprise.' But when she lifts off her basket, it's Handa who gets the biggest surprise. Akeyo, meanwhile, is delighted, because tangerines are her favourite fruit!

Starting-points

The tale offers an opportunity to engage children with thoughts of the wider world in a positive context. Children can gain some first-hand experience of Handa's life by tasting the fruits depicted in the story. It is hoped that, by exploring the story, the children will empathise with Handa and develop the idea that we all have different and special talents, wherever and whoever we are. While noting the differences between Handa's setting and our own, it is especially useful to dwell on the similarities, especially feelings.

Children can be encouraged to contribute information from their own cultural backgrounds. They can sometimes draw parallels with other countries – for example, 'We have roads like that in India' and 'My granny in Pakistan has a goat' are both actual comments made by three-year-olds.

Our starting-point

We introduced the story about Handa as one that was about a special little girl who lived in another country a long way away. Before the story was shown, the children were encouraged to guess what the country might be. Some of them had been abroad on holiday and suggested a range of places, some of them countries and some of them localities, features or resorts. This produced a good opening discussion and revealed what the children knew about the wider world, including their attitudes and misconceptions, which helped us in our planning.

Then they were shown the front cover of the book and asked if they could guess now. Somebody said 'Africa', to which the response was, 'Yes, Handa lives in Africa – but Africa is a huge *continent* that has lots of countries in it. Handa's country is called *Kenya*.'

A large world map was used to illustrate this on an interactive white board and the children were challenged to use the magic pen to 'colour in' the continent of Africa and to find the UK. Then we saw if we could find the continent of Africa on the blow-up globe. This was fun, as we took it in turns to throw the globe to each other and see if we could point to Africa. We also discussed how far away Kenya was and how you might get there. Once we had explored the location, we read the story through.

The children enjoyed predicting what would happen next, and we talked about how Handa's life was different from and similar to ours. 'Is that where Handa lives?' asked one child. 'Does Handa go to school?' asked another, while one child wanted to know if there were lions there.

Productive questions
- Where do you think Handa lives?
- Have you ever been abroad, to another country?
- You've been to Spain? What was it like?
- Can you find … on the map? On the globe?
- Have you been anywhere like the place Handa lives?
- How do you think you would get to Handa's country?
- What do you think Handa's country is like? What makes you think that?
- What is the name of the country where we live?
- How is Handa's life like yours?
- How can we find out more about Handa's life?
- What do you think Handa likes about her life?

> 'Look – I can balance a basket on my head like Handa!'

> I'm going to the well to get some water – will you come with me?

> Handa's lucky that she can just pick fruit when she likes.

Challenges and responses

Teacher-directed challenges

This setting provided opportunities for teacher-directed challenges focusing on:

Identifying special talents that each of us has. For example, Handa is very skilful because she can balance a basket on her head. She is also kind and thinks about her friends.

Development of global awareness and associated language – for example: continent, country, Kenya, grassland, mango, giraffe.

Working together by sharing ideas and helping each other – for example, taking turns to pass plates of sample fruit around, telling others what a fruit tasted like.

Problem-solving: Taste and discuss. Which of Handa's fruits is the juiciest? The tastiest? The sweetest?

The development of exploratory language related to the task – for example: sweet, juicy, tasty, soft, chewy.

Set challenges

As children developed positive connotations of Handa's life through 'fruitful' encounters, we challenged them to work together to make a basket of fruit or print fruit patterns using a range of media and tools, such as paint, sponges, paper (cut into strips for weaving), clay:

- Can you make some fruits for Handa's basket?
- Can you make a basket like Handa's?
- Can you print patterns like those on Handa's or Akeyo's dress?

Child-initiated responses to the setting

In this setting, children had the chance to taste exotic fruits and use their senses. There were a range of comments, for example:

- 'Oh, this makes my tongue go bubbly!'
- 'Has Handa got a television?'
- 'I don't eat fruit at home.'
- 'Does Handa like crisps?'

It was interesting to see several children dressing up and acting out scenes from Handa's life. They tried to balance the basket of fruit on their head. Noticing this, we then put the basket and fruit outside so that children could make use of the space. This became a very popular child-initiated game.

The children painted their own play mat and used this with plastic animals. This play helped to reinforce vocabulary and story sequencing.

Sorting challenge

Having become familiar with the story and the elements within it, the children were given a range of pictures and artefacts (see below) and asked to sort them into 'same' and 'different'. They were asked:

- What things are the same in Handa's life and yours?
- What things are different?
- What do you think makes Handa happy/ sad? What about you?

Resources

- Pictures and captions from the story, e.g. of the different animals and fruits
- Picture of the world from space, e.g. a satellite photograph
- Picture or map showing Handa's country and one showing ours
- Pictures of friends and family, a school, etc.
- Selection of objects, some of which could be specific to Kenya or the United Kingdom and others not – for example, sandals, bucket, basket, cloth, real fruits.

This giraffe's feeling a bit hungry.

I've got the elephant.

We can make a path.

Children's voices

Rebecca: 'I'm going to choose something the same … I'm going to choose … chickens!'

Danny: 'My Nan's got chickens!'

Rebecca: 'And I think I'll have … a dog'.

Danny: 'My Nan's got a dog! And she's got a goat!'

Jessica: 'Has she got an elephant?'

Danny: 'Don't be silly! And I've seen an elephant at the zoo. It's the same!'

Teacher: 'Do you think we would see elephants in our country if they weren't in the zoos?'

Rebecca: 'No, because they don't really live here.'

Danny: 'Why do they put them in zoos then?'

Jessica: 'So we can see them!'

Danny: 'Where do they get them from?'

Teacher: 'Elephants live in the continent of Africa and in another country called India. [shows on the globe] You can tell African elephants from Indian elephants because their ears are nearly the same shape as the continent they live in.' [traces outline of Africa]

Danny: 'Where? Show me … oh, they are a bit the same!' [copies and traces outline]

Jessica: 'I think that Handa's lucky to see elephants where she lives. I wish we could see them every day on the way to school.'

Danny: 'I'm going to put all this fruit in here [the sorting circle for 'same'] because I like fruit and so does Handa!'

Rebecca: 'Handa's got friends and so have I. That's the same.'

Jessica: 'Well, that's lots of things the same then! But, she lives in another country and that's different!'

Teacher: [showing photograph of world from space] 'Yes, that's right. Handa lives in another country. Now, what do you think this is?'

Rebecca: 'That's the world, and it's the same, isn't it?'

Jessica: 'Of course it is, silly – we all live on the world!'

Teacher reflections

'We already had some ideas of the objects, pictures and artefacts that we would include in this game, but some were added after listening to the children's talk. For example, we decided to include the picture of the world because we heard some children say that Handa lived in another world.

'Rebecca was the leader in the game and very confident. Danny had some knowledge of animals because his grandmother had a farm, but was very unsure of differences and similarities and the concept of different places. Through his conversation with Rebecca he became more involved in the game and began to think more deeply. He was willing to change his idea of elephants being 'the same' after the discussion.

'The children were fascinated by the animals, and by chance we realised their interest in the shape of the elephant's ears. The next day we set up a table for the children to make elephant masks, using the shape of Africa as a template for the children to draw and cut out their ears. This proved a simple visual prompt for the identification of the African continent.'

Language

Key vocabulary

journey	walk	route
travel	path	village
start	end	grass
tree	bush	animal
giraffe	elephant	zebra
monkey	ostrich	goat
antelope	chicken	dog
fruit	banana	mango
guava	orange	pineapple
avocado	tangerine	juicy
yellow	green	sweet
tangy	soft	world
continent	Africa	country
Kenya	globe	map
hot	dry	dusty
sunny	basket	woven
kind	passion fruit	
	United Kingdom	

Encouraging children to use the language

'I went on a **journey** to see my **friend**.'

'Handa lives in another **country** a long way away.'

'I like Handa – she's **kind**.'

Language across the curriculum

Personal and social

me	friend	family
life	kind	thoughtful
caring	different	same
clever	talent	

Further activities

Extending the learning environment
- Fiction and non-fiction books that illustrate other places and cultures
- Photo-packs of family life in Kenya
- Different types of globes, world map, and a display incorporating animals and fruits from the story.
- The outline shape of Africa, locating Kenya.
- Home corner set up as part of Handa's village with basket and plastic fruit, dressing-up clothes
- Dressing-up clothes, travel bags and props, e.g. sunglasses
- Real fruits for tasting

- Small world animals and table-sized paper for children to drawn their own scenery
- Small world animals with sand tray for exploratory play.

Role play
As well as props for children to act out Handa's journey, set out a corner as an airport check-in desk where tickets can be bought and passports and luggage checked. The children can choose suitable dressing-up clothes and accessories to pack for their trip.
- What kinds of clothes will you need and why?
- Can you make a list?

Small world play
Using a range of small animals, the children use the sand tray or paint their own floor map to act out scenes and variations of the story.

Urban and rural
Ensure that the resources reflect modern as well as traditional Kenyan lifestyles, and stress that some Kenyans live in modern houses and work in offices.

Using the outdoors
Children can devise their own route outside to tell their own local version of the story – taking a present to a friend.

- What will they take? (What fruits grow in our locality?)
- What landmarks can the children find to mark the journey? (bushes, trees, gate, fence, pond, etc.)
- What birds and animals are there in our locality? (robin, blackbird, cat, rabbit, etc.)
- How will they travel? (walk, pedal car, bike, etc.)

The children work collaboratively to act out their story, and then retell it when back indoors.

Investigating fruit

Using the senses blindfold children and ask them to smell, feel and taste fruit to find out which they have in front of them. Find pictures of what the plant looks like with this fruit growing on it. Where is the seed in the plant? Does it have seeds? How are new plants grown? Why do we need to eat fruit? How does fruit help our bodies?

Sustainable development

Encouraging children to share, take turns and think of others is a vital part of sustainable development. This difficult concept is basically about trying not to waste resources and thinking about other's needs as well as our own. As good practice, have small plastic bins with lids and handles that can be used for all fruit waste, and ask the children to empty them daily into a suitable compost container. Show the children the day's waste and use this for discussion – for example:

- What shall we do with this waste?
- Where does rubbish put out for the dustmen go?
- What do you think happens when we put the leftover fruit in our compost bin?

Talk about healthy food and why we should eat it. See also 'Why won't my seed grow?', pages 44-49.

Counting and sorting

Lots of opportunities for 'mathematics talk' and exploration arise from the story. For example:

- How many fruits have you got?
- Can you show me the biggest/smallest?
- Can you collect seven different fruits?
- One's been taken – how many are left?
- Can you put the orange next to/before/in front of the pineapple?

Circle time

Ask the children to take it in turns to show or tell something they are good at, or ask them to say what somebody else is good at.

Visitors

Find someone who has been to Kenya who will come and do a 'show and tell'. We found someone from World Education Development Group who fascinated the children with a range of beautiful clothes and artefacts.

Aims

- Recall a story in increasing detail, for example by sequencing cards
- Use language to imagine, act out or develop experiences
- Make and use a simple map
- Identify some features, and talk about those features the child likes or dislikes.

Teacher comments

Daniel had drawn a very simple map consisting of a long path surrounded by tall grass and trees. He invited three other children to act out the story with him, using a selection of plastic animals. The children agreed what animals they would be, and reminded each other of the sequence of events. Daniel said he liked the long grass because it would be very good for 'hide and seek'. Chloe agreed and said that she liked the grass on the school field best because you could run fast on it.

Assessment for learning

Assessment evidence for geographical learning can be found throughout the Foundation curriculum, not just within Knowledge and Understanding of the World. Good geography builds on children's natural curiosity and develops enquiry skills through first-hand experience and sensory interaction, clear and varied communication, critical questioning, and the ability to empathise with others. Children should be challenged to:

- Ask relevant questions and suggest how they can find answers
- Make connections – for example, cause and effect
- Share and communicate ideas in a variety of ways
- Use photographs and maps for information
- Think about others and the world around them sensitively.

Opportunities should be taken to assess other areas (where appropriate) of early years development such as language and personal, social and emotional education.

Aims

- Investigate places, objects, materials and living things by using all the senses as appropriate.

Auxiliary comments

Robbie and Beth were talking about the fruit together while they tasted it. First they smelled it, then Beth touched it and said to Robbie 'It's a bit soft, but it smells like a lollipop!' Robbie replied 'Mmm, it tastes good. Handa's lucky that she can pick fruit like this when she wants.'

References and further resources

Aldborough, J. (2002) *Where's My Teddy?* Walker Books.

James, S. (1993) *Dear Greenpeace*. Walker Books.

Hutchins, P. (1993) *The Wind Blew*. Red Fox Picture Books

MacDonald, A. and Fox-Davies, S. (1993) *Little Beaver and The Echo*. Walker Books.

Oxfam staff (1996) *Photo Opportunities: Activities for the primary classroom* (photos around the world). Oxfam and ASE.

Oxfam staff (1996) *Photo Opportunities: Activities for the primary classroom* (photos around the world). Oxfam and ASE.

Phillips Mitchell, R. and Binch, C. (1997) *Hue Boy*. Picture Penguins.

Rosen, M. and Oxenbury, H. (2003) *We're Going on a Bear Hunt*. Walker Books.

Sendak, M. (2000) *Where the Wild Things Are*. Red Fox Picture Books.

Traditional African (1996) 'Listen to the tree bear' in Foster, J. and Thompson, C. *First Verses: Finger rhymes*. Oxford University Press.

Aims

- Look closely at similarities, differences and change
- Understand that people have different needs, views, culture and beliefs that need to be treated with respect.

Parent comments

Ayesha told me all about Handa and the country she lives in. She said that Handa was just like her, with a Mum and a Dad and friends to play with, but that she hadn't got a television. She made me laugh though, because she said that Handa probably didn't mind not having a television because she could see real elephants in her country without going to the zoo.

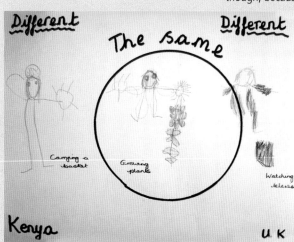

Teacher comments

Ayesha drew a picture of herself and Handa. She explained that she needed a different colour for Handa's skin.

theme: designs for a purpose

the surprise box

It is exciting to lift a lid, open a bag or pull back a cover to reveal the hidden surprise. This theme builds upon children's natural curiosity and desire to investigate what is in closed containers. The activity also supports the development of children's prediction and thinking skills.

Before you start …

Key focus areas

The key focus areas are:

- Mathematics - sorting, size and shape
- Science - materials, weight and skills of prediction
- History - times past
- Design and technology - investigation and evaluation of made products; likes and dislikes; purpose and user.

Essential resources

- Boxes and/or bags to create different versions of the 'Surprise box'
- A wide variety of shoes, including ones for different users and purposes, from different cultures and from times past, made from a variety of materials, and with different fasteners (e.g. laces, buckles).
- Or, other familiar items, e.g. gloves, small toys, plastic tableware, that could fit into containers.
- A range of fabric, paper, card, staplers, glue to join card and fabric, scissors, rulers for making shoes.

Planned outcomes

Children should be able to:

- identify familiar products for a variety of purposes
- listen to others' ideas about, for example, shoes, and offer their own ideas
- talk about what they like or dislike about, for example, shoes
- develop thinking skills, when discussing and evaluating products
- make predictions, through handling the 'Surprise box'
- use technical language with confidence, about shoes, e.g. users and fastenings
- be creative in designing and making.

Shake it!

What's in it?

Careful!

It's noisy when he shakes it.

What can it be?

It can't be big.

Setting up the learning environment

- Make a display of photographs of collections of shoes (labelled with key vocabulary). These photographs should show shoes that are familiar to the children (e.g. trainers), but also ones that are less familiar (e.g. ski boots, clogs). Ensure a good range of users, purposes and materials.
- Set up a Shoe shop in the role-play area (or, if you are looking at books as products, set up a book shop).
- Put out a collection of shoes (real and toy ones) with different fasteners on a table together with books about shoes for children to explore.
- On a table nearby provide writing materials, paper, glue, scissors and shoe catalogues to enable to children to make their own catalogues or shoe pictures.

Starting-points

Young children are naturally curious and want to explore the made world around them. However, this curiosity is sometimes stifled when they are not encouraged, or are even discouraged, from investigating and asking questions. One activity that can be used to stimulate and extend their natural curiosity is to hide what is to be investigated in a container, a 'Surprise box'. This can be used to start the children thinking about possibilities, then to allow them to hold, to smell, to shake, to listen, and then to extend the learning when the object is revealed. By varying the type of container, the children continue to be interested and intrigued by what it might contain. Use a variety of boxes and bags, of different colour, size, shape and way of fastening. Using other products enables you to link the activity to many different themes.

As a health and safety point, remind the children that they should only do this at home with adult permission.

Our starting-point

We used the approach of the Surprise box during our work on looking at the made environment and different products within it. This followed on from a project about the creation of a shoe shop. Many children were fascinated by the variety of shoes that we were all wearing and we looked at colour, ways of fastening, soles, shapes and materials, and thought about why they were different. Some of the children then talked about shoes that they had at home, that other members of their family wore, or their favourite shoes.

Staff and children looked at their shoes and discussed similarities and differences. Children were encouraged to ask the staff questions about their shoes. Photographs of the staff's shoes were taken with the digital camera and printed out, and the children acted as detectives to find the shoes in the pictures.

Each day the teacher put a different shoe in the 'surprise box'. A small group of children handled the box carefully so as not to damage what was inside. They shook it gently, listened carefully, and felt it to see how heavy it was. The children made predictions as to what might be in the box, and were encouraged to give reasons for these.

The role-play area was set up as a shoe shop, and a variety of shoes were placed in it. The children sorted the shoes in a number of ways, including into pairs, those made for different purposes and categorised them as in a real shoe shop. They role-played trying on shoes, having their feet measured and selling the shoes. They also went to the cash desk to pay for the shoes, and could buy polish to keep them looking good.

The shoes were changed regularly. Shoes from different cultures and from times past were included, and the children were encouraged to notice the differences and to suggest reasons for them.

Productive questions

- What kind of shoe is it?
- Does it have a special name? What is it?
- Who might wear these?
- When might you/they wear them?
- How are they fastened? Why is that, do you think?
- Which shoes might go together? Why do you think that?
- Why are they slip-on shoes/boots?
- What material do you think they are made from?
- Why are they made from …?
- Could they be made from other materials?
- Do you like them? Why? Why not?
- Who else might like/dislike them?
- Where is the sole?
- Why does the sole look like that?
- Would we wear these shoes today?
- Can you find a pair of shoes to dance in/play football in/wear outside? Why have you chosen them?

Challenges and responses

Teacher-directed challenges

Catalogues were put out for the children to look through. They were encouraged to cut out pictures of shoes for a number of activities with different focuses. These included:

- their favourite shoes
- shoes for someone else
- shoes for a particular purpose
- shoes they did not like.

They stuck the pictures into books, and we wrote the reasons for the choices they made. The books were then put into the library area and parents encouraged to look at them. This was partly to provide support for parents to help them to build on and develop the questions that the children were being asked.

Large drawings of shoes were displayed and appropriate labels added. The children drew their own pictures and created shoe catalogues that were displayed in the Shoe shop.

They investigated a simple machine to measure feet, and used card and a simple slider mechanism to make one of their own.

Set challenges

As the children examined the shoes, we asked the children to:

- make a pair of shoes for a particular purpose
- draw a pair of shoes that had magic powers. They had to think about what the shoes might help them do.

Child-initiated responses to the setting

Most of the children were excited by the shoe shop. While most had visited one, their knowledge was extended through the role-play. Both boys and girls enjoyed playing in the shop.

The 'Surprise box' kept the interest of the majority of the children. They handled it carefully, as they thought it might hold something precious.

Many of the children role-modelled the 'Surprise box' activity. They put a shoe in the box and asked friends what kind of shoe was in it. Some asked their friends the reasons for their prediction. A few preferred to find their own container, and used some of the questions that the teacher had asked.

Many of the children started to look at shoes in the books that they were 'reading' or during story-time. Some volunteered reasons for different characters to be wearing different shoes.

Language

Key vocabulary

shoe   boot   trainer   pump
slipper   fastener   lace   Velcro
buckle   zip   slip-on   pull-on
user   wear   sole   leather
rubber   plastic   fabric   felt
material   strap   tongue   smooth
slippery   ballet shoe

Encouraging children to use the language

The **sole** is **smooth**.

We need to **tie the laces** to **fasten** the shoe.

I would wear the **slippers** in my house.

A **dancer** would use those **shoes.**

Language across the curriculum

Science

material   wet   waterproof   soft
hard-wearing   smooth   rough
bumpy

Mathematics

big   small   fits   measure   size
bigger   smaller

History

a long time ago   before   after

Children's voices

Teacher: 'Can you guess what's inside the surprise box?'

Aziz: 'Shoe. It's a shoe. Heavy. Big shoe. Shoe for Dad.'

Teacher: 'When might he wear it?'

Aziz: 'He puts it on when he goes out. Lace up. I can't lace up. It is thick. It is bigger than my shoe.'

[The box is taken away and another shoe put in it.]

Prema: 'My turn! It is quiet when I shake. Listen! I think it's a slipper. It is! It is soft, fluffy. It is for my friend. I don't have slippers. It will slip on her feet. It could be red 'cos she likes red.

Teacher: Where do we usually wear slippers?

Prema: 'Indoors … 'cos her feet would get wet in the rain. I think I could bend it.'

Nadia: 'My turn now [goes away and secretly puts a shoe in the box then returns]. Look. I have put a shoe in [offers it to another child]. Think what it is. Shake it – do it carefully. Who will wear it? Why? Is it big? Is it little? You can open it now. What does it look like? How will it do up? Does it have a sole? What does it look like?'

Teacher reflections

'This activity excited almost every child, and built on the majority of the children's experiences. The element of surprise still engaged the children's interest, confirming that using the curiosity of children is one strategy to use to develop learning.

'Questions that develop lower-order thinking skills (see 'Productive questions', page 89) were used to introduce the activity. Questions to develop higher-order thinking skills, such as evaluation (e.g.'What can you tell me about this?) were included as the discussions with the children were developed.

'When playing the game with their friends, some of the children role-played the questions that they had heard during teacher-directed sessions. While some of the children were not at a stage at which they could answer "why?" questions, others listened and then in turn used the questions when playing. It is important to model questions to support learning and to support the development of the children's thinking.

'Most of the children listened well to each other when they were talking about the contents of the box. Some were confident and able to indicate agreement or disagreement with the ideas of others, and a few were able to give reasons for their predictions.

'The children's technical vocabulary was extended mostly when they were handling the shoes, but some children further developed this when searching catalogues for shoes and creating their own catalogues.

'Through investigating and evaluating a range of footwear, the children gained a wealth of ideas about the variety that is available. Some showed creativity when making shoes (e.g. for teddy), through the use of new knowledge that they had acquired.

'It was evident that almost all of the children had extended their technical vocabulary, and many used these words when discussing the shoes or in the shoe shop.'

Barnaby Bear and his Dad put on their walking boots.
'Why do I need big boots?' asks Barnaby.

So you won't slip.

That's why the soles of my boots are like car tyres.

Further activities

Shoe catalogue

The children can create their own 'catalogue' using their drawings, digital photographs that they take, and pictures from catalogues. Labels can be added to highlight particular features of the shoes. Prices could be included.

Make large cut-outs of other types of product, e.g. gloves, mittens, and their possible users and ask the children to match them up.

Displays

- Make a footwear display. This can be changed regularly to include girls' and boys' shoes, indoor shoes, sports shoes, outdoor shoes, adult shoes, shoes from times past.
- Create a display of photographs of the teachers' favourite shoes.
- Display any shoes that the children make, together with a picture of the 'person' whom the shoes are for.
- Put up large pictures of different shoes, and label the parts of the shoes.

Exploration table

- Make a collection of different materials for making footwear for children to handle (e.g leather, laces, rubber, fur).
- Extend the activity by adding a collection of toys from times past for children to handle and play with and match materials to products.
- Make a collection of fasteners which the children can investigate through play (e.g. zips, poppers, Velcro fasteners, laces, buttons).

Stories

- Encourage the children to look at the shoes that characters are wearing in stories. You can ask questions relating to the type of shoe, why they are wearing them, and whether the children like or dislike them. Ask the children to draw alternative shoes for the characters and/or for their favourite story characters.
- Tell stories in which characters need a product, e.g. a basket in 'Little Red Riding Hood'. Let the children choose an appropriate one from a collection displayed in front of them. Ask them for reasons for their choice.

See also 'Can you get to Grandma's safely?' on pages 38-43.

Making shoes

- Ensure that the children have a range of fabrics and appropriate fasteners so that they can make a pair of shoes for a 'person' they choose.
- Use the outdoor environment to extend the children's thinking skills about the different surfaces and which soles or shoe shapes are safest on the play equipment. This could be extended to which footwear is best for different types of weather.

Recycling shoes

Set up a shoe recycling area and ask the children to tell their families and friends about it. (The Council Recycling Officer should be able to advise on this and arrange for the shoes to be collected when the container is full.) This gives children practical experience of recycling and raises all sorts of interesting questions. Where are the shoes going to? What will happen to them? Why would anybody want my old shoes? Let children have the responsibility for making sure that the shoes are in pairs and that an adult is informed when the container is full.

Musical boxes

Make a music box. A box that can be shaken or struck and will make a good sound. Use different 'music boxes' to make the sound effects for a poem or story. Use the 'music box' as the rhythm for a song that they children can sing. What kind sounds can be made? How can we use different materials to make different sounds? How do we make a music box that has a low, high, loud and quiet sound? How can we make a music box that when it is shaken sounds like rain falling?

Visit or visitor

Walk to a local shoe shop, or ask someone from the shop to visit you. Encourage the children to ask questions about the different shoes in stock and why there are so many different types. The visitor might also bring a 'Surprise box'.

Aims
- Show curiosity, observe and manipulate an object.
- Describe simple features of an object.

Teacher comments
Gerald was excited by the box. He shook the box, and was able to determine that 'it sounded heavy'. However, he was very anxious to open the box and see what was inside. Having seen the shoe, he was able to make comparisons in terms of size, 'It's bigger than my foot', colour, and when it might be worn. He said that it was made from 'soft' material and that it would feel nice on your foot. He tried the shoe on, and then left it and moved away.

Assessment for learning

The activities will provide opportunities to assess children's knowledge and understanding of the made world, and of particular products within it. We can assess their thinking and decision-making skills, and ability to investigate and evaluate products, related to user and purpose. There are also opportunities to assess language, mathematics, history and personal, social and emotional development.

References and further resources

Foster, J. (ed) (1993) 'Magic shoes' in *Twinkle, Twinkle, Chocolate Bar*. Oxford University Press.

Grimm, J., Grimm, W., Read, L. and Hurt-Newton, T. (1999) *The Elves and the Shoemaker*. Ladybird Books.

McKee, D. (1993) *Elmer on Stilts*. Red Fox.

Milne, A.A. (1989) 'Happiness' in *When We Were Very Young*. Methuen.

Morris, N. and Stevenson, P. (1990) *A Fun Book of Touch: FEEL!* Firefly Books.

Tanner, G. and Wood, T. (1995a) *In the Street*. A&C Black (familiar designs).

Tanner, G. and Wood, T. (1995b) *Eating*. A&C Black.

Traditional Nursery Rhyme: 'There was an old woman who lived in a shoe'.

Aims
- Investigate an object, by using all the senses as appropriate.
- Talk about what is seen and identify differences.

Teacher comments
Shamina picked up the box with care. She first shook it gently and then harder. She said that the shoe sounded bigger than

hers, but it could not be bigger than the box or it would not fit in. She was happy to explore for longer, and smelled the box. She made a guess that it was not soft as the shoe made a loud noise, but it was not a big boot because it did not make a really loud noise.
When Shamina saw the shoe, she was able to talk about the material it was made from, and thought that a lady would wear it when she went to a party as it was silvery and shiny.

Aims
- Ask questions about how things are designed.
- Find out about and identify some of the features of an object that has been observed.

Auxiliary assistant comments
Lekisha had put a shoe in a box and was modelling the activity that she had taken part in with the teacher. She was careful that no-one saw what she put in the box (a trainer). The other children in the group were interested as she carried it very carefully into the circle of children. She asked different questions and let the other children take turns to handle the box. Through the questions she asked about what materials it could be made of, who could wear it, when would the person wear it, and how it fastened, it was clear that Lekisha had a good understanding of the product.

resources and sources

Teaching and learning resources

Books

Beetlestone, F. (1998) *Creative Children, Imaginative Teaching.* Buckingham: Open University Press.

Bilton, H. (2002) *Outdoor Play.* London: David Fulton Publishers.

Browne, N. (1991) *Science and Technology in the Early Years.* Buckingham: Open University Press.

Bruce, T. (1991) *Time to Play in Early Childhood Education.* London: Hodder & Stoughton.

de Bóo, M. (1999) *Enquiring Children: Challenging teaching.* Buckingham: Open University Press.

de Bóo, M. (ed) (2000) *Laying the Foundations in the Early Years.* Hatfield: Association for Science Education.

Devon Curriculum Services (n.d.) *The Plays Pack: Purposeful learning activities for young scientists.* Devon County Council.

Donaldson, M. (1978) *Children's Minds.* Glasgow: Fontana.

Drury, R., Miller, L. and Campbell, R. (eds) (2000) *Looking at Early Years Education and Care.* London: David Fulton Publishers.

Fisher, R. (1990) *Teaching Children to Think.* Hemel Hempstead: Simon & Schuster.

Hendy, L. and Toon, L. (2001) *Supporting Drama and Imaginative Play in the Early Years.* Buckingham: Open University Press.

Hutchin, V. (1996) *Tracking Significant Achievement in the Early Years.* London: Hodder & Stoughton.

Johnston, J. (1996) *Early Explorations in Science.* Buckingham: Open University Press.

Koshy, V. (2002) *Teaching Gifted Children 4-7: A guide for teachers.* London: David Fulton Publishers.

Mallett, M. (1999) *Young Researchers: Informational reading and writing in the early and primary years.* London: Routledge.

Mallett, M. (2004) *Early Years Non-Fiction.* London: Routledge Falmer.

Matthews, J. (1994) *Helping Children to Draw and Paint in Early Childhood.* London: Hodder & Stoughton.

Merry, R. (1998) *Successful Children, Successful Teaching.* Buckingham: Open University Press

Moyles, J.R. (1996 edition) *Just Playing? The role and status of play in early childhood education.* Buckingham: Open University Press.

Qualifications and Curriculum Authority (2000) *Curriculum Guidance for the Foundation Stage.* London: DfEE/QCA.

Rogers, S. (2003) *Role Play in the Foundation Stage.* London: David Fulton Publishers.

Siraj-Blatchford, J. and MacLeod-Brudenell, I. (1999) *Supporting Science, Design and Technology in the Early Years.* Buckingham: Open University Press.

Toye, N. and Prendeville, F. (2000) *Drama and Traditional Story for the Early Years.* London: Routledge Falmer.

Vygotsky, L. (1986) *Thought and Language.* Cambridge MA: MIT Press.

Wallace, B. (ed) (2002) *Teaching Thinking Skills Across the Early Years: A practical approach for children aged 4-7.* London: NACE/Fulton Publications.

Wood, D. (1992 edition) *How Children Think and Learn.* London: Paul Chapman Publishing.

Journals

Early Years: an International Journal of Research and Development is produced by Carfax/Taylor and Francis for the Training, Advancement and Co-operation in Teaching Young Children (TACTYC) (The Professional Association of Early Childhood Educators) – see website (http://improbability.ultralab.net/tactyc/index.html) or contact: TACTYC, BCM Box 5342, London WC1N 3XX. TACTYC also produces a quarterly newsletter.

Early Years' Matters, a newsletter produced by Learning and Teaching Scotland, is available online (http://www.ltscotland.org.uk/earlyyears matters/). Related links are also provided to support each article. Each issue has a selection of articles relevant to those supporting early years care and education.

Websites

As well as the Subject Association websites listed on page 4, your local education authority should have an area of its website devoted to early years. Other LEA websites may also provide inspiration for your early years work.

There are a number of sites that are devoted to specific early years initiatives (e.g. the Early Years Library Network – www.cilip.org.uk/eyln/) that are well worth looking at. The websites listed below offer free resources and ideas for activities.

The Becta Virtual Teaching Centre (http://curriculum.becta.org.uk/docserver.php?docid=2666) includes materials that provide a framework to help nurseries plan for integrated use of ICT across all subjects of the curriculum and throughout the Foundation Stage.

The Basic Skills Agency's early years pages (www.basic-skills-observatory.co.uk /keydata_content.php?catID=3) include downloadable documents on literacy, numeracy and language in three categories: policy, practice and research.

Early Years Experience site (www.bigeyedowl.co.uk/) is intended to provide free help and ideas to all those involved with young children, including parents and educators in Playgroups, Nurseries or Schools.

The National Literacy Trust (www.literacytrust.org.uk/database/earlyyears. html) includes statistical information and links to sites that focus on specific early years initiatives, as well as practical advice and useful links to other early years sites.

Parent Zone Scotland (www.parentzonescotland.gov.uk/preschool/ preschoolcurriculum.asp) includes links to downloads of the *Curriculum Framework for Children Aged 3-5.*

QCA's early years pages (www.qca.org.uk/ages3-14/160.html) include information on the *Curriculum Guidance for the Foundation Stage* for England.

The Scottish Executive (www.scotland.gov.uk/library5/education/ isey-00.asp) has downloads of the *Early Years Strategy.*

The Teaching Ideas site (http://www.teachingideas.co.uk/earlyyears/ contents.htm) includes a section devoted to Early Years activities – which may provide you with some inspiration.

Sources

Each chapter includes a list of the resources used in the activities, together with alternative storybooks. Extra resources, such as useful websites, are also included. Many storybooks are now available in a range of formats. A search on an internet bookstore (e.g. www.amazon.co.uk) will indicate whether the book you wish to use is available either as a big book, on video or audio tape or as a children's reader. The addresses and contact details for each publisher mentioned are included here.

ABC/All Books for Children
An initiative managed by Reading Is Fundamental (RIF) (RIF is an initiative rather than a publisher). Reading Is Fundamental UK, National Literacy Trust, Swire House, 59 Buckingham Gate, London SW1E 6AJ.
Tel: 020 7828 2435 Fax: 020 7931 9986
E-mail: rif@literacytrust.org.uk
Website: www.rif.org.uk

A&C Black
37 Soho Square, London W1D 3QZ
Tel: 020 7758 0200
E-mail: customerservices@acblack.com

Atheneum
Website: www.atheneum.com (a distributer/importer of books)

BBC Consumer Publishing
BBC Worldwide Limited, Consumer Publishing, Woodlands, 80 Wood Lane, London W12 0TT
Tel: 020 8433 2000 Fax: 020 8749 0538

Bodley Head
see Random House

Cambridge University Press
The Edinburgh Building, Shaftesbury Road, Cambridge CB2 2RU
Tel: 01223 325588 Fax: 01223 325152
E-mail: educustserve@cambridge.org
Website: http://uk.cambridge.org/

**Devon Curriculum Services
(Devon County Council)**
Devon Curriculum Services, Great Moor House, Bittern Road, Sowton, Exeter EX2 7NL
Tel: 01392 385 352
E-mail: edmail@devon.gov.uk
Website: www.devon.gov.uk/eal/acatalog/home.htm

Dorling Kindersley
The Penguin Group (UK), 80 Strand, London WC2R 0RL
Tel: 020 7010 3000 Fax: 020 7010 6060
Website: http://uk.dk.com

Folens
Boscombe Road, Dunstable, Luton LU5 4RL
Tel: 0870 609 1235 or Fax: 01582 673079
E-mail: orders@folens.com
Website: www.folens.com

Frances Lincoln
Bookpoint Ltd, 130 Milton Park, Abingdon Oxfordshire OX14 4SB
Tel: 01235 400 400
E-mail: UKsales@frances-lincoln.com
Website: www.franceslincoln.com

Greenwillow Books
Greenwillow Books, Harper Collins Children's Books, 1350 Avenue of the Americas, New York, NY 10019 USA
Tel: 00 1 212 261 6500
Website: www.harperchildrens.com/hch/aboutus/imprints/willow.asp

Hamish Hamilton Children's Books
see Penguin Books

Hodder Children's/Hodder & Stoughton
Bookpoint Ltd, 130 Milton Park, Abingdon, Oxfordshire OX14 4SB
Customer Service Tel: 01235 400580
Fax: 01235 400500
Website: www.hodderheadline.co.uk/

Houghton Miflin Juvenile Books
Corinthian Court, 80 Milton Park, Abingdon, Oxfordshire OX14 4RY
Tel: 01235 833827 Fax: 01235 833829
E-mail: info@hmcouk.co.uk
Website: www.hmco.com

Ladybird Books
Marketing Department, 80 Strand, London WC2R 0RL
Tel: 020 7010 3000
E-mail: ladybird@penguin.co.uk
Website: www.ladybird.co.uk

Macmillan Children's Books
Brunel Road, Houndmill, Basingstoke Hampshire RG21 6XS
Website: www.macmillan.com

Methuen Young Books
Sales Department, 215 Vauxhall Bridge Road, London SW1V 1EJ
Tel: 020 7798 1605 Fax: 020 7828 2098
E-mail: sales@methuen.co.uk
Website: www.methuen.co.uk

Orchard Books
see Watts Publishing

Oxfam
274 Banbury Road, Oxford OX2 7DZ
Tel 01865 311311
Website: www.oxfam.org.uk/index.htm

Oxford University Press
Great Clarendon Street, Oxford OX2 6DP
Tel: 01865 556767 Fax: 01865 556646
E-mail: enquiry@oup.co.uk
Website: www.oup.co.uk

Penguin Books
Penguin Direct, Pearson Customer Operations, Edinburgh Gate, Harlow, Essex CM20 2JE
Fax: 0870 8505777
Website: www.penguin.co.uk

Picture Lions/Collins Picture Lions
Harper Collins Publishers, 77-85 Fulham Palace Road, Hammersmith, London W6 8JB
Customer Service Tel: 0870 787 1724
Fax: 0141 306 3767
Website: www.harpercollinschildrensbooks.co.uk

Picture Puffin
For all enquiries regarding online book orders
E-mail: PUKCustomer.Service@pearson.com
Website: www.puffin.co.uk

Random House
20 Vauxhall Bridge Road, London SW1V 2SA
Tel: 020 7840 8400 Fax: 020 7233 8791
Website: www.randomhouse.co.uk/intro.html

Red Fox Picture Books
see Random House

Scholastic/Scholastic Hippo
Westfield Road, Southam, Leamington Spa CV33 0JH
Tel: 01926 813910 Fax: 01926 817727
E-mail: enquiries@scholastic.co.uk
Website: www.scholastic.co.uk/

Walker Books
Order through bookshops or www.amazon.co.uk
E-mail: enquiry@walkerbooks.co.uk
Website: www.walkerbooks.co.uk

Watts Publishing Group
96 Leonard Street, London EC2A 4XD
Tel: 020 7739 2929 Fax: 020 7739 2181/2318
Website: www.orchardbooks.co.uk/obidx.htm

Wayland Publishers
Hodder Wayland, 338 Euston Road, London NW1 3BH
Tel: 020 7873 6000 Fax: 020 7873 6024
Website: www.hodderwayland.co.uk

index